Delicious and Nutritious Recipes to Help You Overcome Swallowing Difficulties and Enjoy Food Again with Confidence

Oswald rios

TABLE OF CONTENTS

INTRODUCTION 1

CHAPTER 1: INTRODUCTION TO DYSPHAGIA: UNDERSTANDING THE BASICS 3

- The Effects of Dysphagia on Daily Living 4
  - Impact on the Body 5
  - Social Impact 5
  - Impact on Emotions 5
  - Mental Impacts 5
  - Impact on Caregivers 6
- Why Early Diagnosis and Treatment are Crucial 6
- Evaluation and Testing 7
- Treatment 7
- Early Diagnosis Benefits 8
  - Better Food and Water 8
  - Less Chance of Aspiration 8
  - Easier Swallowing 8
  - Better Speech and Conversations 8
  - Health in Social and Emotional Aspects 8
  - Less Expensive Healthcare 9
  - More Freedom 9
  - Better Living Conditions for Caregivers 9
  - No More Food Intake Complications 9
  - Avoidance of Deadly Conditions 9
  - Better Adherence to Treatment 9
- What Leads to Dysphagia? 10
- Issues Arising 10
- Incidence and Prevalence 11
- Modern Research 12

CHAPTER 2: ANATOMY AND PHYSIOLOGY OF SWALLOWING: HOW IT WORKS 13

- Development 14
- Involved Organ Systems 15
- The Process of Swallowing and Its Functions 15
- Swallowing Mechanism 16
  - Oral Phase 16
  - Pharyngeal Phase 16

Esophagus Phase 18
Influence on Clinical Practice 18
Anatomical 19
Functional 19
Iatrogenic 20

CHAPTER 3: TYPES AND CAUSES OF DYSPHAGIA 21

Different Types of Dysphagia 22
Oropharyngeal 22
Esophagogastric 23
Esophageal 23
Causes of Dysphagia 24
Dry Mouth (Xerostomia) 25
ALS – Amyotrophic Lateral Sclerosis 25
Achalasia 26
Stroke 26
Diffuse Spasm 26
Esophageal Eosinophilia 27
Throat Ring Esophagus 27
Goldflam Disease (Myasthenia Gravis) 27
Multiple Sclerosis 27
Radiation 28
Dystonia and Tremors in Parkinson's 28
Scleroderma 28
Split Palate Lip 28
Cancer of the Esophagus 29

CHAPTER 4: RECOGNIZING DYSPHAGIA: SIGNS AND SYMPTOMS 30

Identifying Dysphagia's Warning Signs 31
Swallowing Pain (Odynophagia) 31
Choking 31
Aching Throat or Chest 31
A Hoarse Voice 31
Food Coughing 32
Unease While Swallowing 32
Chronic Bad Breath 32
Drooling 32
Weight Loss 32
Constant Heartburn 33
Dehydration 33

Food Inhalation — Causing Pneumonia ... 33
Putting off Eating ... 33
Skipping Meals ... 34
Loss of Appetite ... 34
Swallowing-Difficult Kids May Refuse Certain Foods ... 34
Leaking Mouthfuls of Food or Drink ... 34
Burping After Eating ... 34
Irregular Breathing During Mealtime ... 35
Rapid Weight Loss with No Effort ... 35
Which Kids are Most Likely to Get Dysphagia? ... 35
Risk Factors ... 36
Aging ... 36
Substance Abuse ... 36
Smoking ... 37
Other Potential Risks ... 37

CHAPTER 5: DIAGNOSIS & TREATMENT OF DYSPHAGIA ... 38
Why Conventional Treatment? ... 39
Diagnosis ... 39
Videofluoroscopy ... 39
Barium X-ray ... 40
Functional Endoscopic Evaluation of Swallowing (FEES) ... 40
The Swallowing Water Test ... 40
Manometry ... 40
Endoscopy ... 41
Treatments ... 41
Oropharyngeal Treatments ... 42
Esophagus Treatments ... 43
Treatments for Infants ... 44
Brain Damage ... 44
Lip and Palate Dislocation ... 45
Esophagus Constriction ... 45
Tips for Safe Swallowing ... 45
Physical and Mental Condition ... 46
Setting ... 46
Positioning ... 46
Preparing Meals ... 47
Mealtime Tips ... 48
Tips for Drinking Medicine ... 49
After Meal Tips ... 50

Between Meals Tips 51

CHAPTER 6: NUTRITION AND DYSPHAGIA: REQUIREMENTS AND RECOMMENDATIONS 52

Dysphagia Patients' Dietary Requirements 53
Taking a Look at How Well Someone Is Eating 54
Modified Diets 56
The National Dysphagia Diet (NDD) 56
Chopped or Grinded Foods 56
Thickening Liquids 57
Treatment of Dysphagia with Nutritional Supplements 57
Oral Nutritional Supplements 57
Parenteral Nutrition 57
Enteral Nutrition (EN) 58

CHAPTER 7: 100 RECIPES FOR DYSPHAGIA 59

Recipes for Soft Food 61

Recipe 1: Easy, Delicious, and Creamy Scrambled Eggs 62
Recipe 2: Sweet Potato Mash 63
Recipe 3: Soup with Cream of Mushrooms 64
Recipe 4: Fruit and Cottage Cheese Dish 65
Recipe 5: Smoothie Fixins': Peanut Butter and Bananas 66
Recipe 6: Creamy Carrot-Ginger Soup 67
Recipe 7: Creamy Mashed Potato 68
Recipe 8: Baked Sweet Potato Mash 69
Recipe 9: Creamy Risotto with Spinach and Mushrooms 70
Recipe 10: Greek Yogurt and Sweet Potato Mash 71
Recipe 11: Creamy Broccoli Soup 72
Recipe 12: Avocado Egg Salad 73
Recipe 13: Risotto with Butternut Squash 74
Recipe 14: Banana Oatmeal 75
Recipe 15: Baked Oatmeal with Sweet Fruits 76
Recipe 16: Chicken and Rice with Cream Sauce 77
Recipe 17: Creamy Cauliflower Puree 78
Recipe 18: Salmon with Pureed Vegetables 79
Recipe 19: Egg and Avocado Salad 80
Recipe 20: Creamy Rice Made with Cauliflower 81

Recipes for Pureed Foods 82

Recipe 21: Creamy Cauliflower Puree 83
Recipe 22: Pureed Chicken and Rice 84
Recipe 23: Pureed Sweet Potatoes 85
Recipe 24: Apple Puree 86
Recipe 25: Pureed Tuna and Veggies 87

Recipe 26: Pureed Carrot Soup 88
Recipe 27: Pureed Chicken and Rice 89
Recipe 28: Pureed Sweet Potato 90
Recipe 29: Pureed Turkey and Gravy 91
Recipe 30: Banana and Yogurt Puree 92
Recipe 31: Pureed Chicken and Vegetable Casserole 93
Recipe 32: A Rich and Creamy Mushroom Puree 94
Recipe 33: Fruit Puree with Greek Yogurt 95
Recipe 34: Carrot-Ginger Puree 96
Recipe 35: Creamy Butternut Squash Soup 97
Recipe 36: Greek Yogurt & Berry Smoothie 98
Recipe 37: Creamy Broccoli Puree with Cheese 99
Recipe 38: Rich Vanilla Pudding 100

Recipes for Liquid Food 101

Recipe 39: Creamy Potato Soup 102
Recipe 40: Strawberry and Banana 103
Recipe 41: Tomato Basil Soup 104
Recipe 42: Carrot Ginger Soup 105
Recipe 43: Creamy Vegetable Soup 106
Recipe 44: Smoothie with Blueberries 107
Recipe 45: Broccoli Cheese Soup 108
Recipe 46: Banana Pudding 109
Recipe 47: The Broccoli Cheddar Soup 110
Recipe 48: Blueberry Oatmeal 111
Recipe 49: Chicken Noodle Soup 112
Recipe 50: Butternut Squash Soup 113
Recipe 51: Broccoli-Cheddar Soup 114
Recipe 52: Creamy Tomato Soup 115
Recipe 53: Creamy Broccoli Soup 116

Recipes for Solid Food 117

Recipe 54: Gravy-Coated Meatballs 118
Recipe 55: Ground Turkey Meatloaf 119
Recipe 56: Avocado Scrambled Eggs 120
Recipe 57: Roasted Vegetable Puree 121
Recipe 58: Chicken and Rice Casserole 122
Recipe 59: Black Bean and Sweet Potato Bowl 123
Recipe 60: Beef Stroganoff 124
Recipe 61: Chicken with Sweet Potato Mash 125
Recipe 62: Chicken and Rice Casserole 126
Recipe 63: Salad with Shredded Chicken 127
Recipe 64: Red Sauce Meatballs 128
Recipe 65: Slow-Cooked Shredded Chicken 129

Recipe 66: Ground Beef Stroganoff 130
Recipe 67: Stir-Fried Chicken and Vegetables 131
Recipe 68: Mashed Potatoes and Soft Meatballs 132
Recipe 69: Avocado Toast with Soft Scrambled Eggs 133
Recipe 70: Soft Meatloaf 134
Recipe 71: Chicken Pot Pie 135

Recipes for Snack And Desserts 136

Recipe 72: Banana Oatmeal Cookies 137
Recipe 73: Yogurt Parfait 138
Recipe 74: Chocolate Avocado Pudding 139
Recipe 75: Smoothie with Jelly and Peanut Butter 140
Recipe 76: Apple Sauce with Cinnamon 141
Recipe 77: Greek Yogurt with Almonds and Blueberries 142
Recipe 78: Chia Seed Pudding 143
Recipe 79: Baked Cinnamon Apple Chips 144
Recipe 80: Avocado Chocolate Mousse 145
Recipe 81: Soft-Baked Oatmeal Cookies 146
Recipe 82: Mango Sorbet 147
Recipe 83: Soft-Cooked Poached Pears 148
Recipe 84: Chocolate Pudding 149
Recipe 85: Mango Yogurt Smoothie 150
Recipe 86: Fruit Salad 151
Recipe 87: Apple Slices Baked 152

Recipes for Beverages 153

Recipe 88: Strawberry-Banana Smoothie 154
Recipe 89: Chocolate Almond Milk 155
Recipe 90: Creamy Vanilla Shake 156
Recipe 91: Pineapple Coconut Water 157
Recipe 92: Apple Cinnamon Smoothie 158
Recipe 93: Blueberry Green Tea 159
Recipe 94: Vanilla Chai Latte 160
Recipe 95: Orange Creamsicle Smoothie 161
Recipe 96: Iced Herbal Tea 162
Recipe 97: Homemade Sports Drink 163
Recipe 98: Creamy Coconut Milkshake 164
Recipe 99: Carrot Ginger Juice 165
Recipe 100: Creamy Mango Lassi 166

CHAPTER 8: 4-WEEK MEAL PLAN 167

CONCLUSION 174

REFERENCES 175

INTRODUCTION

A warm welcome to the Dysphagia Cookbook! You know how hard it is to eat well and obtain the nourishment you need if you or a loved one has trouble swallowing. By delivering tasty and nutritious dishes that are simple to prepare and digest, this cookbook aims to restore the pleasure of eating.

Dysphagia, or difficulty swallowing, can arise for many different reasons. Dysphagia can develop with age or be brought on by diseases or disorders, including stroke, Parkinson's disease, or tumors. Others may be unable to swallow due to neurological diseases or congenital abnormalities. However it develops, dysphagia harms the quality of life by making eating a chore rather than a pleasurable experience.

But things don't have to be like that at all. The Dysphagia Cookbook is a comprehensive collection of dishes developed with the unique requirements of people with dysphagia in mind. Each recipe's flavor and nutritional value have been optimized without sacrificing swallowability or digestion.

This cookbook is more than just a collection of recipes; it also features valuable information and suggestions for improving the quality of your daily meals. You will gain knowledge of the various forms of dysphagia, how they manifest themselves in eating habits, and the methods and approaches available for dealing with swallowing problems. There are also recommendations for modifying recipes to suit personal tastes and dietary restrictions, allowing you to prepare meals that are just right for you.

The dedication to healthy, tasty cuisine lies at the core of the Dysphagia Cookbook. Nobody should go hungry regardless of their physical condition or swallowing capacity. That's why I've used high-quality, nutrient-rich, and freshly-prepared whole foods in our recipes. The recipes in this book have all been tested for easiness of digestion without sacrificing flavor or nutritional value.

Specialists with significant knowledge and expertise in dysphagia management created the recipes in this cookbook. These specialists include chefs, dietitians, and speech therapists. They know the difficulty in getting tasty and nutritious food for those with dysphagia. That's why they developed a wide range of tasty and simple recipes to digest, so you can indulge in your favorite dishes without feeling guilty. There's something delicious here: a filling breakfast, a soothing soup, or a delicious main course.

This cookbook intends to help you rediscover the pleasure and satisfaction of meal preparation, whether for yourself or a loved one. There is no need for dysphagia to prevent someone from eating tasty, healthy food with a little ingenuity and many flavors. This cookbook's strength lies in its comprehensive coverage of the entire day's eating needs, from breakfast to dessert.

Not only is the Dysphagia Cookbook a useful resource for people living with dysphagia, but it is also a must-have for their loved ones and friends who help them with daily tasks like cooking and eating. This cookbook will give you the information and recipes to make nutritious and delicious food for someone close to you who is having trouble swallowing. There are also suggestions for making mealtime a more pleasant and social experience and providing help with feeding.

Finally, it's important to note that this cookbook isn't just about learning to cope with dysphagia; it's also about learning to love food and eat with gusto. We think everyone, no matter their health, deserves to enjoy tasty and satisfying meals. Therefore, we pay equal attention to our dishes' taste, texture, and appearance as we do to their safety and nutritional value.

To sum up, the Dysphagia Cookbook is an excellent resource for those dealing with swallowing difficulties themselves or providing care for someone who does. It offers a variety of simple-to-digest meals that are also tasty and healthy, bringing additional pleasure to mealtimes. The contributors of this cookbook have high hopes that its readers will be encouraged to take culinary risks and rediscover the pleasures of cooking.

CHAPTER 1

INTRODUCTION TO DYSPHAGIA: UNDERSTANDING THE BASICS

Dysphagia occurs when problems arise in the muscles that control swallowing. When someone has difficulty swallowing, they risk getting food or other debris stuck in their throat or lungs. The epiglottis is a flap that prevents vomit, food, and stomach acid from entering the lungs. When you have dysphagia, this can be a problem. Aspiration is the proper term for this sort of thing. It is dangerous because it frequently results in pneumonia and other complications.

You probably swallow a few hundred times daily without giving it any thought. Everything from meals and liquids to the body's regular production of saliva and mucus is swallowed. Dysphagia can result from difficulties with any part of the swallowing process.

The *pharynx* is the area of the throat where food travels after it has been swallowed. Once the meal reaches the bottom of the mouth, it travels down the esophagus and into the stomach. The muscles along the path must perform a series of actions. In addition to this, it needs synchronization with the muscles used for breathing. When you swallow, there is a brief break in your breathing.

The act of swallowing is intricate. The action calls for the cooperation of many nerves and muscle units. Professionals typically divide the process into three stages:

1. **The oral preparatory stage.** Here, you break down your food into manageable pieces and mush them together so they're easier to swallow. A "bolus" is what you'd name something like this. Food and liquid are stopped at the mouth's arch by the tongue before reaching the pharynx. The next step is moving your tongue upward, forcing the bolus back along the palate and into the upper throat. You are partially in charge of your behavior.
2. **The pharyngeal stage.** Here, your pharyngeal muscles tighten in time with one another. This shifts the bolus toward the lower esophageal sphincter. The esophageal sphincter also loosens up during this time. This is a compact muscle band surrounding the lower esophageal sphincter. That way, the bolus can travel down through your esophagus.
3. **The esophageal stage.** The bolus travels down the throat while the esophageal muscles flex in unison. The muscle at the base of the esophagus loosens up. The lower esophageal sphincter is a compact circle of muscles. This opens the digestive tract for the bolus.

The Effects of Dysphagia on Daily Living

The effects of dysphagia on one's quality of life can be devastating. If you cannot easily and properly swallow food or drinks, this can result in various health concerns, including malnutrition and dehydration. A person's social life, emotional state, and mental health may all be negatively impacted by dysphagia, in addition to the person's physical health difficulties.

Impact on the Body

The most evident and immediate effect of dysphagia is on the body. The slower eating that occurs when someone has difficulties swallowing might increase their feelings of exhaustion and dissatisfaction. Long-term weight loss, starvation, and dehydration are all possible outcomes of dysphagia.

Fear that one might choke or aspirate one's food or drink is a persistent concern for many persons with dysphagia. Anxiety and stress brought on by such apprehension might exacerbate existing problems with swallowing. People with dysphagia frequently avoid particular foods or liquids, resulting in a restricted and typically bland diet.

Social Impact

Dysphagia can have serious repercussions in social settings as well. Because eating is typically done in the company of people, not being able to do so can exacerbate feelings of alienation and loneliness. Many persons with dysphagia have feelings of shame and embarrassment because of their disease. This often causes them to withdraw from friends and family and stop engaging in things they once enjoyed.

Those who struggle with dysphagia may also experience anxiety when eating in a social setting. It's common for people to avoid social situations involving food and drink because they're too afraid of choking or coughing.

Impact on Emotions

Dysphagia can have psychological and social consequences in addition to physical ones. Many people become depressed, frustrated, and angry when they cannot consume their usual food and drink. It might be especially challenging to accept the loss of autonomy and autonomy over one's own body.

Mental Impacts

The cognitive repercussions of dysphagia are real. A constant fear of choking or aspiration might make it hard to concentrate on anything else. This can cause dementia, especially in the elderly.

Impact on Caregivers

Remember that dysphagia has consequences for the caretakers and the person with the disorder. Caregivers must constantly monitor the risk of choking or aspiration; special foods must often be prepared. This responsibility can weigh heavily on the caregiver's shoulders regarding time and emotional energy, especially if the caretaker is a loved one.

Why Early Diagnosis and Treatment are Crucial

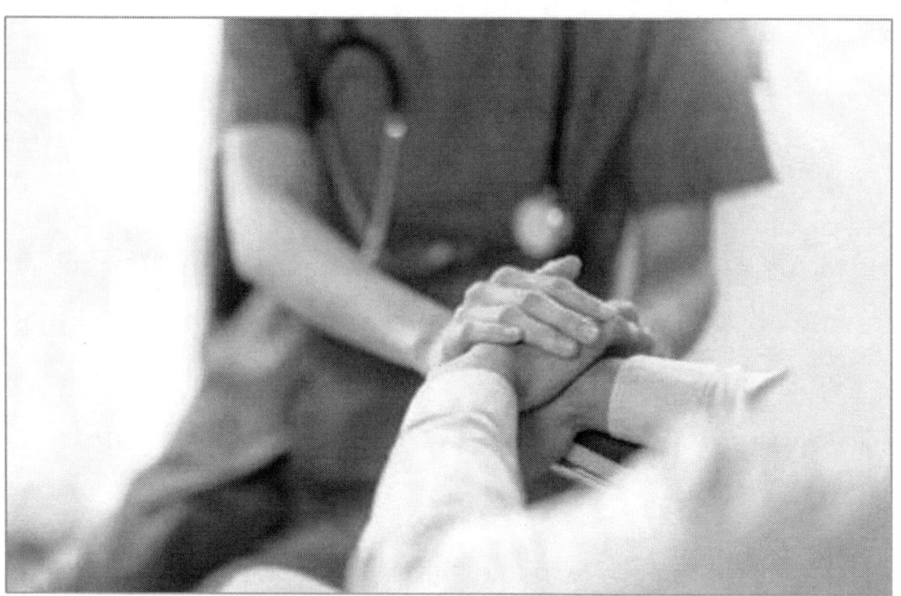

There are many reasons why it's important to catch dysphagia early on. First, getting checked out early can avert further health issues later on. The inability to swallow properly can result in several potentially fatal complications, including starvation, dehydration, and aspiration pneumonia. Early dysphagia detection can reduce the risk of these complications developing.

Secondly, there is an advantage to catching problems early. The sooner dysphagia is diagnosed and treated, the higher the likelihood of a full recovery. Through treatment, swallowing can be bettered, additional injury to the esophagus or airway can be avoided, and quality of life can be enhanced.

Third, there may be financial benefits to finding problems early on. Early diagnosis and treatment of dysphagia can reduce the need for costly medical interventions, including surgeries and emergency department visits. Preventing the need for expensive long-term care is another benefit of early identification.

Evaluation and Testing

Early diagnosis of dysphagia can be achieved through screening and evaluation. Medical personnel can access many screening techniques to identify patients at risk for dysphagia, including questionnaires and tests that may be performed at the bedside. Healthcare providers can use these screening instruments to identify patients who may benefit from additional evaluation and treatment.

Swallowing assessments determine how well a patient can swallow food and liquids. Manometry, video fluoroscopy, and fiber-optic endoscopy are tests that may be included in a comprehensive evaluation. These evaluations can be useful in pinpointing the root of dysphagia and establishing a treatment strategy.

Treatment

The best way to treat dysphagia varies depending on what causes it and how bad it is. Dysphagia can occasionally be transient and go away on its own. In other circumstances, treatment may be required to enhance swallowing function and forestall more difficulties.

Some possible ways to treat dysphagia are:

- **Diet changes:** Making food and drinks smoother or thicker can make them easier and safer to swallow.
- **Exercise and therapy:** Some exercises and treatments can help strengthen the muscles used for swallowing and make it easier to swallow.
- **Medication:** Some medicines can help people with dysphagia swallow better or treat conditions that cause dysphagia.
- **Surgery:** Surgery may be needed to treat dysphagia, but this is rare.
- **Utilization of Adaptive Resources:** Feeding tubes and customized utensils can aid those with dysphagia in securely consuming food and liquids.

Early Diagnosis Benefits

When treating dysphagia early can help the patient in many ways. Let's have a look at a few of the most crucial ones:

Better Food and Water

People with dysphagia may struggle to eat a balanced meal and drink enough water. Early care can ensure that patients get enough to eat and drink, which is important for their health.

Less Chance of Aspiration

Aspiration pneumonia, which can be life-threatening, can happen when food or liquid gets into the lungs because of dysphagia. Early care can cut down on the chance of aspiration and keep problems from happening.

Easier Swallowing

With the right care, people can improve their ability to swallow, improving their lives. They can eat and drink what they like without worrying about choking or aspirating.

Better Speech and Conversations

Dysphagia can make it hard for people to speak and communicate, making it hard for them to say what they want. Early treatment can make it easier to swallow, which can help with speech and conversation.

Health in Social and Emotional Aspects

Dysphagia can make it hard to make friends and feel good about yourself, leading to loneliness and sadness. Early care can help people keep their social lives and stop mental health problems from starting.

Less Expensive Healthcare

Savings in both patient and medical care budgets can be realized by the early detection and treatment of dysphagia, which can assist in reducing complications and hospitalizations.

More Freedom

Dysphagia can make it hard for a person to eat and drink independently. Early treatment can make swallowing easier for people and help them recover independence.

Better Living Conditions for Caregivers

Dysphagia can also affect the quality of life of the people who help people with dysphagia take care of themselves and do things for them. Early treatment can make caregiving easier and improve the caregiver's quality of life.

No More Food Intake Complications

Dysphagia can make it hard to eat and drink, which can cause many health problems. Early care can stop these problems from happening and help people stay healthy.

Avoidance of Deadly Conditions

Dysphagia can cause people to choke or aspirate, which can be fatal. Early treatment can lower the chance of these problems, making people safer and making it less likely that there will be an emergency.

Better Adherence to Treatment

People are more inclined to accept interventions when treating dysphagia early because their situation isn't as bad. Treatment success rates and general health may increase as a result.

What Leads to Dysphagia?

When there is a disruption in the brain regulation or the structures of the swallowing process, this is called dysphagia. If the muscles in your tongue or cheeks are weak, shifting food around in your mouth may be challenging so you can chew it. If you have had a stroke or have another problem with your nervous system, it may be hard to start your swallowing reaction.

This signal tells the body to safely move food and liquids through the throat. Another problem can arise if the muscles in the throat are too weak to properly convey the food down to the stomach, as can happen following cancer surgery. Esophageal problems can also cause trouble swallowing.

Dysphagia's reasons will be discussed in more detail in Chapter 3.

Issues Arising

Dysphagia can be a big problem. A person who has difficulty swallowing may not be able to get enough of the nutritious nutrients they need to keep their weight in a healthy range.

Food bits too big to swallow can get stuck in the throat and make breathing hard. People with dysphagia often find that clearing their throat or coughing isn't enough to eliminate food or liquid entering their airways. Aspiration pneumonia can occur if food or liquid gets stuck in the airway and enters the lungs, providing a breeding ground for bacteria that cause lung infections.

When you have trouble swallowing, you may also get a hole outside of your esophagus because the wall of your esophagus is weak. This strange pocket holds some of the food that is being swallowed. When someone with this problem lies down or sleeps, they may pull leftover food into their throat. Food might get stuck in the esophagus if it is too thin. This could block your stomach's entrance, making consuming additional food or beverages impossible.

Incidence and Prevalence

Dysphagia is a widespread condition that can strike anyone at any time. About 8% of the general population has some kind of dysphagia, and the number of people who have it increases as they age (Bhattacharyya, 2014).

Prevalence means how many people have a certain disease or situation at a certain time. Researchers have found that millions of people around the world suffer from dysphagia. In the U.S., for example, up to 15 million people are thought to have dysphagia, and most of these people are adults over 50 (Bhattacharyya, 2014). Dysphagia is even more common in some groups, like people with neurological diseases, head and neck cancer, or other health problems that affect how the body swallows.

The term "incidence" describes the rate at which new cases of any specific illness or health problem emerge during a given time frame. It's hard to know how often dysphagia happens, but we do know that it gets worse with age and becomes more prevalent in some groups. For example, between 37% and 78% of stroke patients have trouble swallowing, based on how severe the stroke was and where the brain damage was (Bhattacharyya, 2014).

The rate of dysphagia in patients diagnosed with neck and head cancer can range anywhere from thirty percent to one hundred percent, based on the stage of the disease and the tumor's location.

Dysphagia is more common as people get older and can be caused by many different medical problems and other causes. Medications that weaken the swallowing muscles are one example of a lifestyle choice that can raise the risk of dysphagia. Environmental factors, such as smog and exposure to toxins, can also cause dysphagia.

Dysphagia is a common problem with catastrophic consequences, although it is not usually an indicator of something more serious. Dysphagia is often caused by something small, like acid reflux or a small infection, and can be fixed with the right treatment.

Early identification and treatment of dysphagia can improve results and quality of life, so you must talk to a doctor if you're having trouble swallowing. In a nutshell, millions of individuals all over the world suffer from dysphagia, a disorder that is frequently misdiagnosed.

Modern Research

Researchers are working to enhance the diagnostic and therapeutic options available to medical professionals for swallowing difficulties. People of all ages, with and without dysphagia, are being examined in terms of every component of the swallowing process so that researchers can better understand the differences between normal and disordered processes.

Safer methods of studying the tongue and throat in motion while swallowing has also been developed thanks to research. These strategies will aid doctors and SLPs in conducting risk-free evaluations of their patients' improvement during treatment.

Researchers are learning more about why some treatments work for some patients but not others due to studying different therapy modalities. Thanks to this knowledge, some people may be spared life-threatening lung infections, while others will be spared tube feedings.

CHAPTER 2

ANATOMY AND PHYSIOLOGY OF SWALLOWING: HOW IT WORKS

The ability to swallow is critical to our survival. The act is so routine that we hardly give it much thought. But have you ever given any thought to how it works? Swallowing involves many different muscle groups and nervous system pathways working together to accomplish what needs to be done.

When you swallow, your tongue, esophagus, and throat all work together to complete the task. The backside of one's mouth and the esophagus are connected through a coordinated effort between the tongue and the throat. Muscular contractions in the esophagus move anything you're trying to eat or drink down to your stomach.

Swallowing is a difficult procedure, although it happens automatically as a reflex. However, swallowing might become problematic or even impossible for some people. Numerous circumstances, such as neurological disorders, anatomical irregularities, or injury to the relevant muscles, can contribute to this.

Medical personnel caring for patients with swallowing disorders must thoroughly understand swallowing's anatomical and physiological foundations. When medical professionals thoroughly understand the process, recognizing and treating swallowing issues improves patient outcomes.

In this chapter, we'll explore the many mechanisms involved in swallowing, from the anatomical to the physiological. We'll look at the muscles and bones that play a role and the neurological circuits that command the process. If you're interested in finding out more about this vital biological process, come along on the journey with us!

Development

It is intriguing to learn that learning to swallow starts very early in a person's life. Research has shown that the ability to swallow begins to form as early as 15 weeks of pregnancy. Amniotic fluid volume regulation is fascinating because it is important for the fetus's healthy development.

Babies' swallowing abilities develop gradually over the first few years of life. Babies start to develop conscious control of their swallowing as they are exposed to various meals. As they move from a liquid to a solid diet, this procedure is crucial to their health and well-being.

Notably, the sequence of sucking, swallowing, and breathing greatly impacts how the swallowing mechanism develops. This sequence grows more refined as infants develop and learn to better coordinate their movements. Sucking, swallowing, and breathing are complicated motor skills that require early training of many different muscle groups and neural circuits in the brain.

Furthermore, learning how to swallow does not stop in infancy. It's a never-ending cycle that varies and adapts to your lifestyle, nutrition, and health status. Dysphagia occurs when the muscles used for swallowing deteriorate due to aging. Therefore, proper dental hygiene, regular exercise, and a nutritious diet are critical for healthy swallowing.

Involved Organ Systems

Several muscle groups and anatomical features work together to allow us to swallow. Food and liquids are transported from the mouth to the stomach by numerous muscles originating in the mouth, pharynx, larynx, and esophagus. Swallowing is a complex procedure that relies on many different muscles all working together to prevent injury. Regular exercise and checkups are important to keep those muscles strong and healthy.

The Process of Swallowing and Its Functions

There are generally agreed upon three phases of swallowing, and these are oral, pharyngeal, and esophageal. Both solids and liquids go through the pharynx and the esophagus. However, there are some subtle differences in the oral phase of swallowing when boluses are processed and transported into the oropharynx. Together, these steps ensure that a bolus reaches the stomach while keeping aspiration out of the picture.

Swallowing Mechanism

Oral Phase

There are typically two phases to the oral phase:

1. Preparatory

The preparation phase involves placing the bolus of liquid food between the front of the tongue and the back of the hard palate to create a seal in the oral cavity. The bolus remains open when solid food is chewed and otherwise worked on in the mouth.

2. Propulsion

The bolus is pushed back into the oropharynx by lifting the tongue. This mass remains within the oropharynx until that either becomes consolidated by recurrent cycling or the pharyngeal phase begins.

Pharyngeal Phase

All of the activities above can be attributed to voluntary muscular control. The pharyngeal phase starts when the bolus gets to the palatoglossal arch. This is the first step in the eating process that can't be undone. The stimulation is carried to the single tract nuclei in the brain by afferent sensory fibers originating in the oropharynx. Later, efferent muscle fibers move to innervate the laryngeal, pharyngeal, and esophageal muscles to orchestrate a reflex reaction. There are two main goals for this phase:

1. Transports eaten items to the esophagus.
2. Keeps harmful substances from entering the lungs.

A series of coordinated stimuli, lasting for about a second, begins as the food bolus enters the esophagus and terminates when the UES closes around the bolus.

Nasopharynx Closing

The pharyngeal phase starts when the levator palatini and tensor palatini pull the soft palate up. This seals the nasopharynx and keeps pressure from leaking into the nasal passage.

Preserving the Airway

The pharyngeal phase is responsible for guarding the airway through the coordinated physiologic reaction known as swallowing apnea, in which breathing stops throughout the swallowing process to prevent aspiration. This apneic period, which typically lasts about 0.5 to 1.5 seconds and tends to stop the exhalation stage of breathing, avoids aspiration while the individual is breathing in. Vocal fold closure is the body's principal defense against aspiration.

Inhibiting the resting contraction of the posterior cricoarytenoid and stimulating the lateral cricoarytenoids to adduct the cords. The oblique and horizontal arytenoid muscles pull the arytenoid cartilage in tandem, which helps close the glottis. At the same time, the arytenoids are brought forward to touch the epiglottis and help open the airway leading to the esophagus. Although the tongue's retroversion of the epiglottis is not actively involved in airway safety, it does help guide the food bolus through the piriform fossa and down the throat.

Hyoid-laryngeal Elevation

By contracting the suprahyoid muscles, the pharynx is lifted and dragged anteriorly, facilitating the opening of the pharyngeal-esophageal transition.

Transfer of Bolus

The bolus is pushed downward by sequentially contracting the upper, center, and lower pharyngeal constrictor muscles from the top down. Food boluses are steered toward the upper esophageal sphincter (UES) by a wave of pressure generated by a fast activation and contraction sequence in the pharyngeal muscles. Amazingly, the speed ranges from 20 to 40cm/s. The pharyngeal phase is irreversible because once it begins, it acts in an "all or nothing" fashion, like a reflex.

Crossing the UES in Transit

The pharyngeal phase concludes when the food bolus passes through a patent upper esophageal sphincter (UES) and into the esophagus. When at rest, the sphincter stays in a state of tonic contraction to keep air out of the esophagus; however, it opens through a series of three distinct mechanisms:

1. The sphincter opens when the thyrohyoid muscle contracts, which causes the larynx and hyoid to migrate superiorly and anteriorly.
2. Relaxation of the cricoid cartilage using manometry.
3. The bolus causes a pressure-dependent dilatation of the UES.

Esophagus Phase

As soon as it enters the esophagus, the bolus is accompanied by an influx of peristalsis, which causes it to go inferiorly. This phase, like the pharyngeal one, occurs automatically and is not governed by a will. It is substantially more sluggish at a speed of only 3–4 cm/s than the pharyngeal phase. Once the bolus has passed the LES and entered the stomach, this stage is complete. The lower esophageal sphincter (LES) is toned-contracted during rest to block stomach acid reflux and relaxes during swallowing.

Influence on Clinical Practice

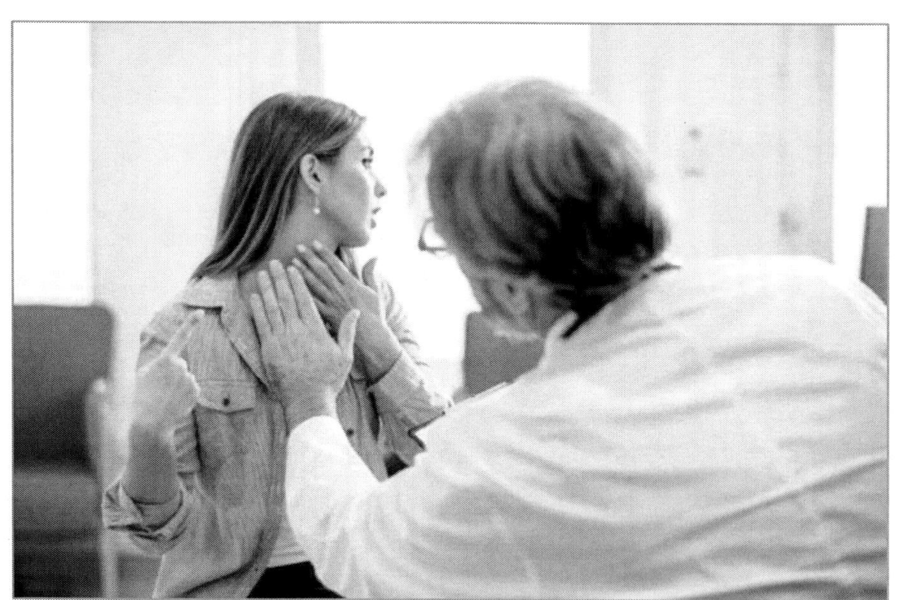

The clinician's ability to diagnose dysphagia relies heavily on their knowledge of swallowing physiology. Dysphagia can be brought on by problems with any of the swallowing process's steps, which might have anatomical, functional, or iatrogenic origins.

Detailed histories are more accurate than other diagnostic tools in determining the etiology of dysphagia (80% of the time), even though research like barium swallows, electromyography, and endoscopies can help doctors. Symptoms of oropharyngeal pathology include a history of coughing and choking when swallowing, a sense that food is lodged in the throat, or trouble starting the swallowing process.

If these signs and symptoms are present, a barium video-radiographic examination of the oropharynx may be warranted to rule out oropharyngeal dysfunction. The presence or progression of symptoms and difficulties swallowing solids or liquids are additional criteria for diagnosing esophageal dysfunction. To rule out esophageal causes of dysphagia, endoscopy is usually necessary.

Anatomical

Examples include pharyngeal and esophageal obstructive pathologies, such as strictures and sphincters. Most esophageal strictures can be traced back to reflux. The treatment consists of expanding the affected area using a balloon and inhibiting proton pumps so the condition does not return. The outpouching of a hypopharyngeal muscle wall that has become weak causes a Zenker diverticulum.

This pouch can trap food for later regurgitation, which can cause choking and bad breath. Furthermore, the doctor must be aware of extra- and intraluminal malignancies that might cause or contribute to blockage in the gastrointestinal tract. Symptoms like dysphagia and weight loss can proceed more rapidly in these cases.

When the sucking reflex is thrown off during the oral phase, as with a cleft or lip palate, nasal regurgitation and sinus infections become more common. Esophageal atresia is yet another birth defect. Early surgical treatment helps children avoid infections and get a head start on healthy feeding habits.

Functional

Strokes, malignancies, and neurogenic genetic illnesses, including cerebral palsy and amyotrophic lateral sclerosis, are among the most common causes of dysphagia. Poor bolus transfer and aspiration might result from weak or uncoordinated muscular action. Swallowing problems are another symptom of developmental delays, as these individuals often have trouble communicating. Dysphagia rehabilitation helps patients build muscle and gain control over their swallowing mechanisms. Feeding tubes are sometimes used in extreme circumstances to provide proper nutrition.

Multiple factors contribute to the prevalence of esophageal dysfunction. A thorough physical examination can detect connective tissue illnesses like scleroderma and CREST syndrome. Dysphagia, or difficulty swallowing, can occur with solid and liquid foods when the LES cannot relax, as in achalasia. When the cricopharyngeus cannot expand fully, it might cause problems in the upper airway.

Intermittent dysphagia can occur when the peristaltic action within the esophagus is disrupted by dysmotility or spasms. Myotomy, in which a small incision is made in the sphincter to lessen the tonic contraction, and drugs that help relax the muscles are also viable treatment choices.

Iatrogenic

The role of medical care providers in causing dysphagia should not be discounted. Patients undergoing rehabilitation who have undergone surgery on their tongue, pharynx, vocal cords, or other tissues surrounding it that cause direct harm to the swallowing mechanism or threaten airway protection may need to find temporary or permanent alternate nutrition alternatives. Radiation is another potential cause of stenosis and stricture development.

Pill esophagitis, which typically manifests as sudden chest discomfort, is another condition doctors should know about. Medications like doxycycline, alendronate, and nonsteroidal anti-inflammatory drugs (NSAIDs) are just a few examples. If discontinuing the treatment is impossible, switching to a less corrosive formulation is recommended to prevent additional harm.

CHAPTER 3

TYPES AND CAUSES OF DYSPHAGIA

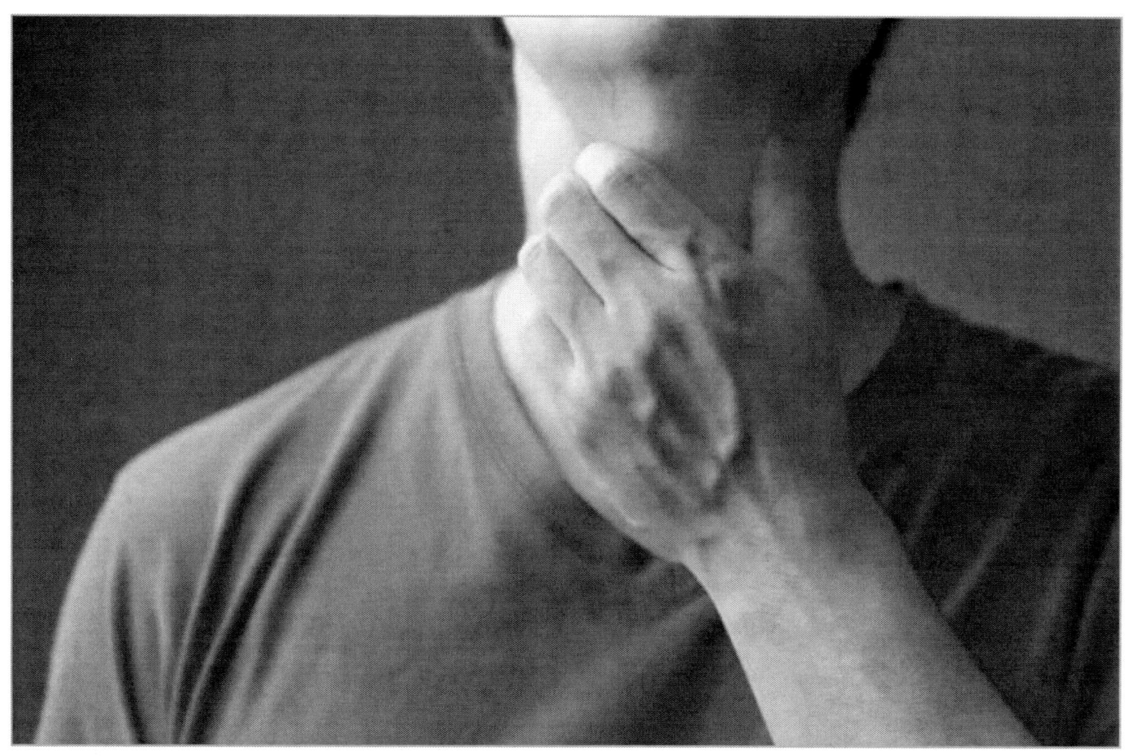

It's easy to swallow, right? Wrong. Unless you are a newborn or a goldfish, you have probably felt the horrible pain of food passing through the wrong pipe. Drinking water while laughing is dangerous, so let's not go there. If your food takes an unplanned detour instead of going straight into your stomach, you may be experiencing dysphagia. This chapter will examine the many kinds of dysphagia and what causes them. Don't worry; I'll ensure it digests like the steak you had the other night.

Dysphagia can be brought on by a wide range of illnesses, some of which include multiple sclerosis, Parkinson's disease, stroke, and muscular dystrophy, to name just a few. Drugs and structural abnormalities in the mouth or throat can also cause dysphagia.

Each subtype of dysphagia has its own particular set of signs and triggers. The best treatment for dysphagia can only be determined once the specific type of dysphagia being experienced is known.

Discomfort or pain during swallowing, a sensation that food is stuck in the throat, coughing or choking when eating or drinking, and regurgitation are all indications of dysphagia. These symptoms can range from annoying to debilitating, depending on the individual.

Different Types of Dysphagia

People of any age can experience dysphagia, brought on by various medical issues. It is important to know what kind of dysphagia a person has so that the right treatment plan can be made for them.

Below, we'll discuss the different kinds of dysphagia and what makes each unique. Different kinds of dysphagia include:

- Esophageal Dysphagia
- Oropharyngeal Dysphagia
- Para-Esophageal Dysphagia
- Esophagogastric Dysphagia

Dysphagia can be classified by the area of the digestive tract it affects and the specific reasons and symptoms accompanying it. It's essential to know the different kinds of dysphagia if you want to treat this disease well. By having a thorough awareness of the many forms of dysphagia, medical personnel may better meet the requirements of their patients and improve their way of life.

Oropharyngeal

Oropharyngeal dysphagia is when it is hard to move a mouthful of food from the mouth to the neck of the esophagus. Normal oropharyngeal swallowing involves coordinating food movement from the mouth to the pharynx and then quickly moving the bolus to the upper stomach. Symptoms involve having trouble with the first step of transporting a bolus of food, whether it be solid or liquid. It's possible that pulmonary aspiration symptoms, such as a feeling of food becoming stuck in your throat or mouth, could fall into this category.

This dysphagia is usually caused by neuromuscular problems, accounting for about 75% to 85% of cases (Wolf, 1990). These problems can also be caused by the way the oropharynx is built. Most of the time, the upper esophageal valve isn't working right. This dysfunction can ensue if the upper esophageal sphincter cannot relax or if its relaxation is not coordinated with pharyngeal contraction.

Esophagogastric

Esophagogastric dysphagia happens when there is a motor or physical blockage that makes it hard for food to move from the lower esophagus sphincter into the fundus of the stomach. Causes include problems with the lower esophageal sphincter, cancerous strictures of the distal esophagus, and benign or mass lesions of the stomach cardia. Achalasia is characterized by hypertension from the esophageal sphincter at the lower, which results in dysphagia due to insufficient relaxing of the sphincteric muscle adjacent to the distal esophagus and stomach. It feels like food is stuck at the bottom of the chest.

Other signs of motility disorders can include odynophagia and chest pain from strong esophageal contractions that don't move food forward. When gastric cardia is damaged in a large enough way, food can't go to the stomach as easily as it should. Para-esophageal dysphagia develops when the esophagus wall and lumen are physically impinged upon or when the esophageal wall is infiltrated, resulting in obstruction.

If this happens a lot, it may change how the stomach moves. Unlike oropharyngeal pain, which is confined to the area around the throat, esophageal pain has a six-dermatomal distribution and can manifest anywhere in the chest.

Esophageal

Eating and drinking can be challenging for those who suffer from esophageal dysphagia because of problems with the esophagus's muscular sphincter. It happens when this part of the stomach moves in a way that isn't normal or when the passageway is physically blocked. Normal esophageal peristalsis isn't fully known, but it needs smooth coordination between muscle contractions in one segment and muscle relaxations in the segments next to it.

Even though the symptoms are caused by problems with how food moves through the esophagus, they will depend on what caused the esophageal trouble. People with trouble moving around will have trouble swallowing liquids and food. There is no shortening of the esophageal lumen, and the esophagus is not squished.

Whether there is an imbalance in the frequency, duration, intensity, or timing of muscle contractions, or all four, a person is diagnosed with a motility disorder. Therefore, dysphagia may accompany spasms (disorganized contractions) or chest pain (powerful, high-pressure contractions).

When physical blockage causes dysphagia, it's always harder to swallow solids than liquids, and it happens sooner. When the esophagus lumen is less than 12 mm in size, patients often experience solid-food dysphagia symptoms. Once the esophageal lumen is reduced by 50% or more, dysphagia for liquids might occur simultaneously with the onset of dysphagia for solids or later.

Causes of Dysphagia

Causes of dysphagia range from neurological abnormalities to medical diseases to bad habits. The correct diagnosis and treatment of dysphagia require understanding its underlying causes. Some of the most prevalent reasons for dysphagia are discussed below; these include brain injury, radiation therapy, esophageal cancer, and Parkinson's disease.

Dysphagia has many potential causes; identifying these causes is essential to designing successful treatments and serving patients better. Insights gained here will be helpful whether you're a healthcare provider, someone with the condition, or a caregiver trying to understand dysphagia and its causes. Some potential reasons for dysphagia are:

Dry Mouth (Xerostomia)

When saliva production is inadequate, a dry mouth results. Medications' unwanted side effects, lack of water intake, and medical illnesses, including Sjögren's syndrome, are the only potential culprits here. Dysphagia occurs when it is difficult to eat because of a dry mouth. Medication to boost saliva production and behavioral adjustments, like drinking more water and utilizing over-the-counter saliva replacements, may be used to treat dysphagia brought on by dry mouth. Diagnosing and treating xerostomia improves oral health and the risk of developing dysphagia.

ALS – Amyotrophic Lateral Sclerosis

Several medical diseases, including ALS (Lou Gehrig's disease), can lead to the development of dysphagia. ALS is a progressive neurodegenerative disease that equally affects people of all ages, races, and genders. It's a degenerative disease that slows down bodily functions by damaging spinal and brain nerves.

Swallowing can become difficult as the muscles involved in swallowing weaken due to ALS. This can be extremely painful and potentially deadly due to the increased risk of choking.

The progressive nature of ALS makes it difficult to treat, and there is no cure. Dysphagia and other problems of ALS are difficult to live with, but they can be managed with various treatments. Dysphagia can be managed with speech therapy and dietary support, while other symptoms of ALS can be treated with medication and other interventions.

Although dealing with ALS is difficult, it is possible to enhance the quality of life with early diagnosis and therapy. People with ALS can maintain their faculties and live fulfilling lives with proper medical care and monitoring.

Achalasia

Achalasia is characterized by a failure of the lower esophageal muscle to relax sufficiently, which prevents food from entering the stomach. Because of this, you may have pain during swallowing or have trouble doing it altogether. Effective management of achalasia is crucial because of the potential for long-term weight loss and malnutrition. Medication, lifestyle adjustments, and surgical procedures are among the ways doctors can help someone with achalasia feel better and live longer.

Stroke

In the elderly population, stroke is the major cause of dysphagia. When the blood supply to the brain is interrupted, brain cells die from a lack of oxygen. Damage to the brain cells responsible for swallowing might cause a person to have trouble doing so. This can be extremely painful and potentially deadly due to the increased risk of choking. Dysphagia caused by a stroke can be treated with speech therapy and changes to the diet, such as making food and liquids easier to swallow by changing their structure and consistency.

Diffuse Spasm

It's a disorder in which you have trouble swallowing because your esophageal muscles spasm in a disorganized way. Ineffective management can lead to unpleasant symptoms like chest pain, unease, and the feeling of choking. Medication, relaxation methods, and dietary changes have all been shown to be effective in treating the symptoms of diffuse spasms and enhancing patients' quality of life.

Dysphagia has many potential causes, including achalasia and diffuse spasm, and understanding these causes is essential for designing effective treatments for those who suffer from this disorder. Healthcare providers can better assist patients in managing their symptoms and increasing their standard of living if they focus on determining and treating the underlying cause of their dysphagia.

Esophageal Eosinophilia

Inflammation of the esophagus caused by an abundance of eosinophils, a kind of white blood cell, is known medically as eosinophilic esophagitis. These cells multiply uncontrollably and invade the digestive tract, causing nausea, vomiting, and diminished swallowing ability. Eosinophilic esophagitis can cause heartburn, a sore throat, and difficulty swallowing. Eosinophilic esophagitis can be treated with medicines to lower inflammation, changes to the patient's diet, or surgery to relieve pain while enhancing the quality of life.

Throat Ring Esophagus

A narrowing of the esophagus, known as an esophageal ring, can make swallowing difficult, especially when eating solid foods. As a result, you may experience pain and have trouble chewing and swallowing food effectively. Causes of esophageal rings include inflammation, scarring, and acid reflux. Medication for acid reflux, dietary adjustments, and surgical treatments are all ways to treat esophageal rings and help the patient feel better. Treating people with dysphagia requires an in-depth familiarity with the conditions that cause it, especially stroke and esophageal ring.

Goldflam Disease (Myasthenia Gravis)

Myasthenia gravis is also referred to as the "Goldflam disease." A lack of strength in voluntarily controlled muscles is a hallmark of this disorder. The issue originates from incorrect nerve stimulation of muscular contractions. The immune system essentially launches an assault on the receptors that act as the intermediaries between the nervous system and the skeletal muscles. Because of this, muscles grow weak and tired, making swallowing difficult. Medications and, in extreme circumstances, surgery can alleviate the symptoms of myasthenia gravis, an autoimmune illness.

Multiple Sclerosis

It's an autoimmune disease that assaults the central nervous system and destroys the protective layer of myelin that lines the nerves. Damage to the nerves that regulate the throat muscles can impair one's ability to swallow effectively. Dysphagia due to MS can be treated with speech therapy, dietary changes, and medicines for symptom management and slowing disease.

Dysphagia is a challenging illness to treat. Therefore, it's important to investigate potential reasons, including Eosinophil esophagitis and multiple sclerosis.

Radiation

Radiation therapy to the head and neck can harm swallowing muscles and tissues, causing difficulty swallowing for the patient. Depending on the extent of the damage, this may cause temporary or permanent dysphagia. Medication, dietary modifications, and rehabilitation exercises are all possibilities for treating radiation-induced dysphagia.

Dystonia and Tremors in Parkinson's

Motor skills are negatively impacted by Parkinson's disease, a degenerative neurological condition. The loss of brain cells that produce dopamine is at the root of this disease. When dopamine levels drop, the body loses the ability to regulate its motions, resulting in tremors, stiffness, and coordination problems. Dysphagia occurs when Parkinson's disease affects the muscles used for swallowing. Dysphagia due to Parkinson's disease is often treated with a multipronged approach, including pharmaceuticals, dietary modifications, and speech therapy.

Scleroderma

Those affected by scleroderma, a series of extremely rare autoimmune disorders, have a hardness and tightness of their connective tissues and skin. Dysphagia can develop when the esophagus is compromised because transferring food and drinks from the oral cavity to the gastrointestinal tract becomes difficult. Medication, surgery, and behavioral modifications, like eating smaller more frequently, may all be part of the treatment plan for dysphagia brought on by scleroderma.

Split Palate Lip

Cleft palates and cleft lip-to-noses come from the improper fusion of the bones of the face and skull during development. Problems with speech and eating may follow from this condition. Surgery to close the opening in the lip or palate is one option, but therapy for speech and dietary changes can also help patients with lip and palate clefts learn to swallow properly. People born with a cleft lip or palate can learn to swallow and talk more clearly with medical professionals' help.

Cancer of the Esophagus

A malignant tumor forms in the esophagus. Drinking and smoking, as well as GERD, are common risk factors for this disorder. Dysphagia happens when cancer blocks the throat, making it hard to swallow. Chemotherapy, Surgery, palliative care, and radiation treatment may be used to treat dysphagia brought on by esophageal cancer. Treating this condition aims to improve the patient's quality of life. Esophageal cancer survival rates significantly improve when diagnosed and treated early.

CHAPTER 4

RECOGNIZING DYSPHAGIA: SIGNS AND SYMPTOMS

The theme for this chapter is mouthfuls. I don't just mean the subtitle, "Knowing the Signs and Symptoms of Dysphagia." Instead, we'll be learning all about dysphagia or trouble swallowing.

The question on your mind right now is probably, "Dysph-what-now?" But have no fear; I'll explain everything in plain English. Put aside that meal, take a deep breath, and come with me as we delve into dysphagia's intriguing (and often humorous) realm!

To treat dysphagia, a doctor may prescribe medication, perform surgery, or have the patient participate in rehabilitation activities to enhance their swallowing function. Let's take a look at some of the most typical Dysphagia symptoms.

Identifying Dysphagia's Warning Signs

The following are some signs that you may be suffering from dysphagia:

Swallowing Pain (Odynophagia)

Dysphagia is characterized by odynophagia or pain during swallowing. It can happen anywhere from the mouth to the stomach because of inflammation, infection, or injury. Experiencing pain when swallowing, also known as odynophagia, should prompt a visit to the doctor to rule out more serious causes.

Choking

Choking is another sign of dysphagia, which occurs when anything goes down the wrong pipe. Because it can cause breathing difficulties or even death, choking is considered a medical emergency. Get medical help immediately if you or someone you know begins to choke while eating or drinking.

Aching Throat or Chest

When trying to swallow, patients with dysphagia may feel that something has become stuck within their throat or chest. Some different things, such as acid reflux, nervousness, or muscle tension, brings on the Globus sensation. This symptom warrants a visit to the doctor because it may indicate a more serious health issue.

A Hoarse Voice

Hoarseness, a change in speech tone or quality, can be a symptom of dysphagia. Keep your vocal cords closed to avoid getting food or fluids into your lungs while you swallow. The vocal cords can become irritated or inflamed if food or liquid becomes stuck in the airway due to dysphagia. A hoarse or even lost voice may result from this. Consult your doctor if you've been experiencing hoarseness to get to the bottom of it.

Food Coughing

Dysphagia manifests itself in several ways, one of which is the tendency to cough up whatever is being swallowed. The cough reflex kicks in to help clear the airway when this occurs. It's crucial to consult a doctor if you cough up food frequently; this symptom may indicate a more serious problem.

Unease While Swallowing

In its early stages, dysphagia is often characterized by episodes of gagging or coughing during swallowing. When swallowing is difficult due to dysphagia, the body reacts by gagging or coughing to prevent choking. If you have trouble swallowing, including gagging or coughing, you should see a doctor to find out the cause and get treatment.

Chronic Bad Breath

Halitosis, or bad breath, can be an indication of dysphagia. Odors might result from the decay of food or liquid lodged in the esophagus. Also, medical problems such as GERD, which can cause dysphagia, can result in chronic bad breath. Consult a medical professional if you have persistent foul breath to properly address the problem.

Drooling

Drooling is a common symptom of dysphagia due to the inability to control saliva production. Some neurological disorders can weaken the muscles responsible for swallowing and saliva control, making this a prevalent problem. Talking to a doctor about your drooling can help you determine what's causing it and get it under control.

Weight Loss

Dysphagia can cause weight loss if it prevents you from getting the calories and fluids your body needs. Dysphagia makes it harder to swallow, which can cause a person to lose weight unintentionally. If you suddenly lose weight, it's crucial to talk to your doctor because it could indicate something more serious.

Constant Heartburn

Heartburn or acid reflux that occurs frequently may be a sign of dysphagia. Stomach acid can make its way back into the throat whenever the muscles at the bottom are weakened or relaxed improperly. This results in a burning feeling in the chest and the neck. Dysphagia is a symptom of gastroesophageal reflux disease (GERD), which is a more serious ailment that can be indicated by chronic heartburn.

Dehydration

Dysphagia can make it hard to swallow, which can lead to dehydration. Dry lips, dark urine, and weariness are all signs that you aren't getting enough fluids in your system. Elderly people are more likely to get urinary tract infections or kidney stones if dehydrated.

Food Inhalation — Causing Pneumonia

Aspiration, the unintentional inhalation of food or fluids during swallowing, is a potentially fatal complication of dysphagia. It is possible to get a lung infection like pneumonia if food or liquid enters the airways and irritates and inflames them. Coughing, wheezing, difficulty breathing, and chest pain are all possible signs of aspiration. Seek emergency medical treatment if you encounter any of these symptoms.

There are several symptoms besides trouble swallowing that may indicate dysphagia.

Because of these experiences, a person could experience:

Putting off Eating

Dysphagia sufferers may stop eating altogether due to the pain and difficulty they experience when attempting to do so. Getting treatment for dysphagia immediately is crucial to prevent malnutrition and other consequences.

Skipping Meals

Some people with dysphagia avoid eating altogether because they are embarrassed by the condition. Getting treatment for dysphagia is crucial because it can cause subsequent issues, including losing weight and malnutrition if left unchecked.

Loss of Appetite

Loss of appetite is a common symptom of dysphagia because of difficulty swallowing. Because of the serious health risks associated with dysphagia, prompt treatment is essential.

Swallowing-Difficult Kids May Refuse Certain Foods

Foods that are hard to swallow or could cause choking may be avoided by children with dysphagia. Because of this, people may have trouble getting enough of the right kinds of food, which might stunt their growth and development. A doctor or feeding therapist can help parents or caregivers develop a healthy eating plan for the child.

Leaking Mouthfuls of Food or Drink

Having food or fluids escape from the mouth is another sign of dysphagia in kids. This can happen before, during, or after a meal, and it might cause you to cough or even choke. The youngster may feel ashamed and isolated, particularly in social settings involving food. Helpful strategies for parents and caregivers include providing the kid with smaller, more often meals, introducing thicker beverages, and helping the child swallow and chew carefully.

Burping After Eating

Another symptom of dysphagia among kids is regurgitation, defined as the uncontrolled throwing up of food or drink when eating or drinking. Several reasons, such as the weak throat or esophageal muscles, gastric reflux, or anatomical irregularity, can contribute to this problem. Depending on the cause, medication, nutrition therapy, or surgery may be necessary for treatment.

Irregular Breathing During Mealtime

Dysphagic children may also have trouble breathing while eating, which is a potentially life-threatening sign in and of itself. This condition can be brought on by aspiration, which is breathing in food or fluids into the lungs; if left untreated, this can progress to pneumonia. If a kid has difficulty breathing while eating, the child's parents or other caretakers need emergency medical help.

Rapid Weight Loss with No Effort

Because of their challenges with eating and swallowing, children with dysphagia may lose weight unintentionally. Especially if the kid is underweight, to begin with, or has an illness that necessitates proper nourishment, this can be a major cause for concern. Parents or caregivers must collaborate closely with a physician or food counselor to provide a healthy and balanced diet to help the child thrive.

Which Kids are Most Likely to Get Dysphagia?

The following medical conditions increase the risk of a kid developing swallowing difficulties:

- Having a preterm birth
- Lip or palate cleft
- Esophageal compression due to external forces

- Overbites and other dental issues
- Delays in development
- Disorders of nerve and muscle function
- Eosinophilic Esophagitis (an esophagus-affecting allergy)
- Acid reflux in the stomach (also known as GERD)
- Big tongue
- Big tonsils
- Craniofacial abnormalities (or birth defects that affect the face, mouth, and throat)
- Developmental issues with the gut system
- Facial and/or vocal nerve paralysis
- Throat lumps and tumors
- Having something, like a coin, lodged in the esophagus which can be very distressing.
- Having a tracheostomy or a surgically created passageway in the neck through which one can breathe.
- Long-term use of a breathing aid (ventilator) which can cause oral sensitivity and vocal cord irritation in children.

Risk Factors

Aging

Presbyphagia is the age-related loss of muscular and nerve strength that might impair one's ability to swallow normally. Dysphagia results from this, leading to serious health issues like starvation, dehydration, respiratory infections, and aspiration if left untreated. Dysphagia in the elderly can be caused by several factors, including dental issues, drug side effects, and medical diseases such as strokes, Parkinson's disorder, and dementia. Elderly people and their caretakers must be aware of the warning signals of dysphagia to get appropriate medical intervention.

Substance Abuse

Heavy drinking has been linked to problems like dysphagia and nerve damage in the throat, which make swallowing difficult. The irritation of the esophagus caused by alcohol consumption might also increase the likelihood of developing Gastroesophageal Reflux Disease (GERD). In addition to raising the danger of choking and aspiration, alcohol's drowsy effects can make it harder to control the muscles used in swallowing. Health issues can be made worse by the nutritional inadequacies that result from chronic alcohol usage.

Accidents and falls are common causes of Traumatic Brain Injury (TBI) caused by the impact of a blow to the head. Dysphagia and other long-term consequences can occur regardless of the injury's seriousness. Rehab and therapy sessions regularly can assist in restoring swallowing ability and enhance the quality of life.

Smoking

Dysphagia is just one of the many health problems from smoking. Cigarette smoke contains chemicals that can inflame and scar the throat and esophagus, wreaking havoc on the muscles and tissues. Smoking also increases the risk of gastroesophageal reflux disease and throat cancer, leading to dysphagia. Loss of appetite, diminished taste and smell, and malnutrition are all possible outcomes of smoking.

Other Potential Risks

There are various risk factors for dysphagia, not just getting older, smoking, or drinking too much. Dysphagia is more likely to occur in people who have suffered a stroke, have head or neck cancer, or have neurological abnormalities. Dysphagia can also be caused by the side effects of drugs, particularly tranquilizers and muscle relaxants, which weaken the muscles used in swallowing. It can also be caused by oral health issues, such as poor dental hygiene, tooth loss, or poorly fitting dentures.

Lastly, being overweight and leading a sedentary lifestyle raises the risk by raising the prevalence of illnesses like gastroesophageal reflux disease and cardiovascular disease, which can damage the esophagus and create swallowing difficulties. To lessen the likelihood of having dysphagia and its problems, it may be able to address these risk factors through changes in lifestyle, medical therapy, and other treatments.

CHAPTER 5

DIAGNOSIS & TREATMENT OF DYSPHAGIA

If you've ever tried to swallow a piece of pizza and felt like it was taking the long way to your stomach, you may have had dysphagia. If you've ever felt that way, you know how annoying it can be to the point of embarrassment. Don't worry, though, fellow eaters! In this chapter, we'll explore the many methods of identifying and treating dysphagia so that you can enjoy your favorite foods without worry. In that case, delve right in!

Why Conventional Treatment?

Dysphagia can significantly influence a person's quality of life, making early diagnosis and treatment all the more important. Early discovery and appropriate illness therapy can prevent future complications and improve overall health outcomes.

Specialists in speech-language pathology, gastroenterology, otolaryngology, and radiology should all be consulted for an accurate diagnosis and effective treatment of dysphagia. Dysphagia can be difficult to diagnose and treat without first determining the root reason and the extent of the problem.

Dysphagia can be diagnosed using any one of numerous accessible methods. Swallowing function tests, endoscopy, imaging examinations, and medical history evaluations may all be part of the diagnostic battery. Once a diagnosis has been made, various treatments may be available, each with pros and cons depending on the condition's root cause and severity.

Depending on the severity of the condition, dysphagia treatment may include a mix of dietary changes, exercise regimens, pharmaceutical management, and even surgical procedures.

Diagnosis

Discuss your symptoms and their onset with your doctor. A physical examination will be performed, and the doctor will examine your mouth for any signs of abnormalities or swelling. Only more specialist tests may reveal the root of the problem.

Videofluoroscopy

The swallowing process can be evaluated with an X-ray test called a videofluoroscopic swallowing examination. A speech-language pathologist administers the test and involves swallowing various radiopaque-dyed meals. This aids in diagnosing swallowing disorders caused by muscular weakening and dysfunction. Images of the mouth, throat, and esophagus are captured in great detail during the examination.

Barium X-ray

Barium X-rays are commonly used to examine the esophagus for abnormalities or obstructions. In this test, you'll drink or take a tablet containing a dye that'll show up on an X-ray of your stomach. The physician or technician will examine the X-ray of your esophagus as you take the drink or medication to assess its functionality. This will aid in the detection of any irregularities or vulnerabilities.

Functional Endoscopic Evaluation of Swallowing (FEES)

The patient's swallowing ability is evaluated during this operation. The doctor can use this instrument to evaluate the consistency of various foods and liquids. This will let the doctor evaluate the extent of your swallowing problems and prescribe the appropriate treatment.

The Swallowing Water Test

Evaluation of a patient's swallowing skills can be done rapidly and easily with the water swallow test. Healthcare providers can assess a patient's swallowing function by monitoring the time and number of swallows necessary to consume a set volume of water. Aspiration is a life-threatening complication that can lead to breathing problems, which helps to recognize its danger. The test is not conclusive, but it does help healthcare providers determine what kind of treatment and interventions are needed to boost swallowing ability.

Manometry

Manometry is a diagnostic procedure used to measure the efficacy of the esophageal muscles and their synchronization during the swallowing process. A thin, sensor-equipped tube is inserted into the esophagus via the nose or mouth to monitor muscular pressure. The efficiency with which the stomach's muscle transport food or liquid can be evaluated with this test. Manometry is a noninvasive outpatient procedure that typically takes 30-45 minutes. Dysphagia can be diagnosed, and appropriate treatment options can be planned using this test, commonly used in conjunction with others.

Endoscopy

A doctor will do an endoscopy to determine if a patient has dysphagia or a swallowing condition. During this procedure, the doctor will place a flexible, thin tube into the patient's mouth and down their throat into their throat to look for any abnormalities. Sedation is sometimes used when a hard tube is used instead. To further investigate potential causes, the doctor may do biopsies of esophageal tissue. Endoscopy is a simple, noninvasive diagnostic that can be performed in about 30 minutes as an outpatient. The information it provides can aid in diagnosis and therapy planning.

Treatments

You may undergo one of several treatments designed to improve swallowing function. If you have trouble swallowing, you may need treatment for either oropharyngeal (a problem in the mouth and throat) or esophageal (a problem in the food pipe) dysphagia.

When selecting how to treat or manage dysphagia, it is important to consider the underlying reason. Some causes of difficulty swallowing can be alleviated by addressing the underlying condition; for example, oral or esophageal cancer. A multidisciplinary team may coordinate treatment for dysphagia, including a speech-language pathologist (SLP), dietitian, and possibly a medical professional.

Oropharyngeal Treatments

When the underlying cause of oropharyngeal dysphagia is neurological, treatment options are limited. This is because drugs and surgery rarely help these conditions. Oropharyngeal dysphagia is treated in three major ways to ensure the patient's safety during eating and drinking:

Therapy for Swallowing

Dysphagia patients can benefit greatly from undergoing swallowing therapy. Professionals in speech-language pathology (SLPs) can tailor a treatment plan to address your specific needs related to eating and swallowing. As part of this process, you may be instructed in swallowing exercises and advised on enhancing your current swallowing skills.

Your speech-language pathologist may recommend dietary adjustments or the use of adapted equipment to help you cope with dysphagia in addition to exercises. If you work with a speech-language pathologist (SLT), you may be able to improve your swallowing skills and return to enjoying your meals again. If you think swallowing therapy could help you, talk to your doctor.

Dietary Modifications

People with dysphagia may benefit from a dietary shift. A dietician can help you develop a diet that is both healthy and easy to swallow. An SLT can guide what to eat and how to eat safely, including taking smaller portions and holding one's head and neck in the right position. They can ensure a pleasant and secure dining experience and may suggest specialized tools.

Tube feeding

Feeding tubes can help patients with trouble swallowing get the nutrition and fluids they need to live. Having the tubes implanted surgically or through a tiny tube via the nose or mouth may be slightly uncomfortable. The patient's condition determines the sort of feeding tube used. Their use necessitates the involvement of a multidisciplinary healthcare team that includes a doctor, speech-language pathologist, dietician, and specialized nurse.

Using feeding tubes carries many hazards and difficulties; thus, the decision should never be made without consulting a medical specialist. Having a feeding tube placed can also facilitate the intake of other medications. Tubes for ingesting food come in two varieties:

A nose tube inserted into the stomach is called a nasogastric tube.

1. A PEG tube, or percutaneous endoscopic gastrostomy, is a tube surgically placed into the stomach through an incision in the skin.
2. Nasogastric tubes are intended for temporary insertion. After roughly a month, the tube needs to be changed out and moved to the other nostril.

PEG tubes are intended for prolonged usage and can last months without being changed. A PEG tube is preferred by those with difficulty swallowing since it can be concealed. However, they have a higher risk of mild problems than nasogastric tubes, including skin infection and blockage. Infection and bleeding inside the body are two significant side effects that might be associated with PEG tubes.

Esophagus Treatments

Following are some treatments for this illness:

Medication

Medication may be an option for treating esophageal dysphagia, depending on the underlying cause. Proton pump inhibitors (PPIs), typically used to treat indigestion, may also alleviate symptoms brought on by esophageal stricture or scarring.

Surgery

In most instances, surgical intervention is the best option for treating esophageal dysphagia.

Botox

When the esophagus muscles become overly tight, a disease called achalasia develops. In some cases, Botox can be used to treat this issue. Muscles that have contracted to the point where food cannot enter the stomach can be paralyzed using Botox. However, you'll only enjoy the benefits for around a year.

The Stenting Process

Because there is a greater possibility of esophageal perforation during endoscopic dilatation, stent insertion is the treatment of choice for patients suffering from esophageal cancer who cannot undergo surgery.

To perform the treatment, a mesh-like metal tube (stent) is inserted into the throat under X-ray or endoscopy supervision. The stent then expands to make the esophagus more spacious for meals. Maintaining the health of your stent requires that you stick to a strict diet.

Dialysis by Endoscope

When the esophagus becomes blocked or scarred, endoscopic dilatation can be used to relieve the symptoms of dysphagia. An endoscope (a tiny pipe with a camera and light) expands the esophagus by passing an inflatable balloon or bougie into the restricted area. Although the treatment can be performed with minimal sedation, there is a remote possibility that the esophagus will be torn or perforated.

Treatments for Infants

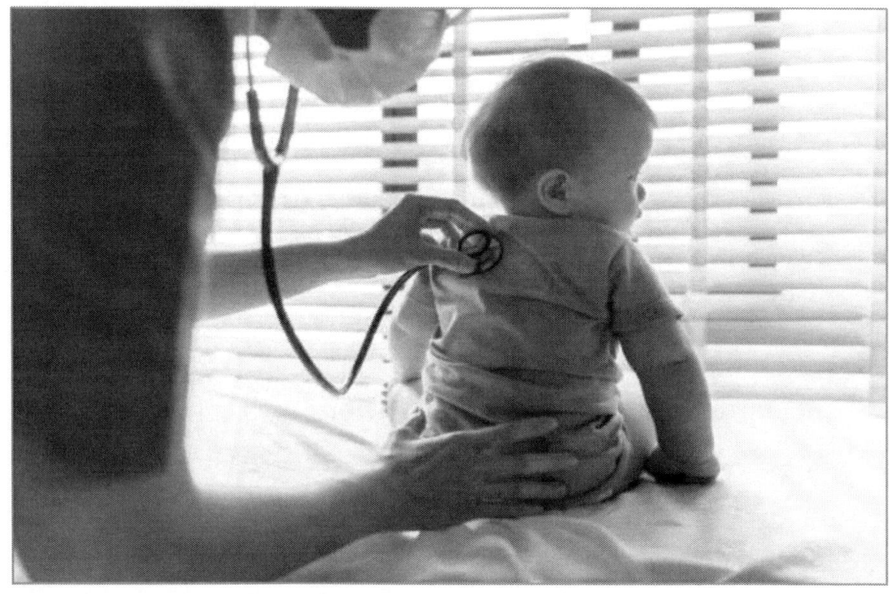

Congenital dysphagia refers to a condition in which a baby is born unable to properly swallow solid foods due to the following conditions:

Brain Damage

Children with cerebral palsy are more likely to have problems swallowing, which can lead to malnutrition and dehydration. A speech-language pathologist (SLP) can assist by teaching safe swallowing skills, making recommendations on food texture, and advising the use of feeding tubes, if necessary. An SLT should engage closely with parents and provide them with practical and psychological assistance.

Lip and Palate Dislocation

A cleft lip or palate is a congenital abnormality that can make it difficult to eat and drink. Surgical correction entails closing the defect in the lip or palate and reconstructing the afflicted area. Depending on the severity of the illness, a multidisciplinary healthcare team may be necessary to address feeding and swallowing issues. The infant may need to undergo additional procedures as he or she develops.

Esophagus Constriction

When the esophagus becomes too narrow, a doctor may perform a treatment called dilatation. An endoscope is inserted into the throat to treat a constricted esophagus, and a balloon is inflated. It's possible that repeating the process will be necessary to get the desired outcome. The patient will be closely watched for issues and given detailed instructions on what and how to eat after the operation. While the esophagus is healing, a feeding tube may be needed. Alterations to one's way of life may also be suggested to stop the constriction from happening again.

Tips for Safe Swallowing

People tend to take ingesting for granted till it starts to be problematic or dangerous for them to do so. Dysphagia and other swallowing difficulties make even the most basic activities of daily living difficult, if not dangerous, for those affected. Safe swallowing can be encouraged, and the danger of aspiration, choking, and other difficulties lessened using a few straightforward methods.

Dysphagic people can eat and drink more comfortably and easily if they alter their diet, improve their posture, and apply other tactics. Here we'll look at some of the best ways to ensure a relaxed and trouble-free ingesting experience.

Physical and Mental Condition

- **Don't eat if you're tired, unsure of yourself, or irritable**: It's better to hold off on eating until you feel more attentive and focused than now if you feel sleepy, confused, or agitated. Aspiration and choking are risks that can occur when a person's attention is elsewhere, and these conditions can make that difficult.
- **Don't eat if you're especially weak or short of breath**: If you do, your body may have trouble coordinating the muscles needed to swallow. Choking or aspiration are also possible outcomes of eating when in this condition. Resting and regaining strength and normal respiratory patterns before eating is recommended to improve swallowing safety.

Setting

- **Turn off the radio, the television, and the cell phone to reduce distractions**: It can be challenging to concentrate on the work at hand if there are interruptions while one is eating. People who eat with minimal interruptions (no TV, radio, or mobile phone use) are less likely to choke or aspirate their food.
- **Listen to relaxing music**: While minimizing disruptions is crucial, listening to music that's easy on the ears can be a welcome addition to a pleasant dining experience. Enjoy a more relaxed and enjoyable lunch with the help of some soothing background music.
- **Shut doors to quiet the dining area**: Limiting foot traffic and noise levels is recommended during mealtimes. A distraction-free zone is ideal for safe swallowing, and you can establish one by closing doors and restricting the number of individuals in the room.
- **Don't force someone to laugh or talk too much when eating**: Mealtime banter and hilarity are great additions to any meal, but too much of either can cause distraction and make it harder to chew and swallow safely. Finding a happy medium between talking with others and focusing on your food is best to avoid choking or aspiration.

Positioning

- **Maintain proper posture**: It is crucial to maintain proper posture when eating to ensure safe swallowing. This means sitting up straight instead of leaning back or slouching. When you sit up straight, your airway is opened, and it's easier to get liquids and foods down your throat. Slouched or slumped postures make choking and aspiration more likely, making swallowing more difficult.

- **Stabilize the body by supporting the legs firmly, making swallowing easier**: Without proper leg support, a person may have dizziness and difficulty focusing on swallowing. Maintaining a secure and comfortable eating position is greatly enhanced by having one's legs firmly supported.

Preparing Meals

- **Getting the person with trouble swallowing involved in the cooking process might increase saliva production and overall appetite**: The patient's saliva production can be increased and their appetite piqued by having them participate in the cooking process. This can increase the person's involvement in swallowing, contributing to safer swallowing.
- **Make sure that neither the meal nor the liquid is painfully hot nor cold by doing a temperature check**: Foods and liquids that are too hot or cold might irritate the throat, making choking and aspiration more likely. Before serving, always do a quick temperature check to ensure the food and drinks are at an appropriate temperature.
- **You should avoid meals that are hard to chew and swallow, such as uncooked vegetables, entire nuts, and peanut butter**: If you have trouble swallowing, eating meals that are particularly hard to chew or swallow might be dangerous. Avoid these and instead go for foods that are easier to swallow, including soups and stews.
- **Avoid sugary pastries and other crumbly snacks**: Choking and aspiration are more likely to occur when eating crumbly, flaky meals or sweet sweets. Avoid these and instead go for foods that are easier to swallow, including soups and stews.
- **Be wary of carbonated drinks**: Carbonated drinks should be consumed cautiously (or avoided entirely) due to the increased risk of choking and aspiration they provide. It's best to use caution around or completely abstain from certain drinks.
- **Be wary of foods with various textures, such as some fruits and cereals with milk**: Choking and aspiration are both made more likely by consuming foods with varying consistencies. It's crucial to be conscious of this fact and select foods with uniform consistency.

- **Be wary of melting foods, such as ice cream and Jell-O**: Fast-melting foods pose a greater choking and aspiration risk because they are more difficult to manage in the mouth. You should use caution with these foods or select something more substantial.
- **Avoid certain foods**: If a certain meal or liquid has caused problems, it is best to avoid it in the future. This will help lower the chance of gagging or aspiration.
- **Provide appetizing foods**: Provide foods that are both delicious and of proper consistency to increase the individual's interest in eating and facilitate safe swallowing. Pureed, blended, or softened options that retain flavor and appeal are included.
- **It's a good idea to thicken liquids**: Liquids should be thickened for those with trouble swallowing to prevent choking and aspiration. To ensure that a liquid is at a safe and acceptable consistency, it is essential to follow the recommendations for thickening it.

Mealtime Tips

- **Eat slowly**: You can enjoy your food and reduce the danger of choking by chewing each bite completely.
- **Eat small amounts at a time**: It's simpler to swallow if you break up your meal into smaller portions and drink in between.
- **Be sure to chew your food thoroughly**: If you chew your meal thoroughly, you can break it down into smaller bits that are easier to swallow.
- **Don't eat while you're talking**: When you talk and eat, more food can go down the wrong pipe, which can lead to choking.
- **Follow the directions for the chin-tuck maneuver**: By bringing the chin into the chest as you swallow, you can close the airway and reduce the risk of food getting into your lungs.
- **Clear your throat**: To be sure the last mouthful of food has been safely taken, try clearing your throat with a light cough and then swallowing again.
- **Don't keep food in your mouth**: Avoid having food build up in your mouth by waiting until you've finished swallowing before loading your spoon or fork again.
- **Make sure no medication or food remains in the mouth after swallowing**: If you check your mouth after you swallow, you can avoid choking from accidentally swallowing food.
- **Remove remaining food**: Removing any remaining food or debris from the mouth using the tongue, hands, or a mechanical suction device is important to avoid choking or aspiration.

- **Use drinks between solids**: This will help move the bolus along and flush out any leftover food. If you're having trouble getting your food down your throat, try mixing solids with liquids.
- **Watch for signs of exhaustion**: If required, finish eating later. People with trouble swallowing may need to stop eating if they are exhausted from trying to chew and swallow their food.
- **Eat several small meals instead of one big meal**: It could be easier for anyone with trouble swallowing to eat several smaller meals throughout the day than one or two big ones.
- **Take note of any coughing, spitting out, choking, gagging, tears, a runny nose, nasal regurgitation, or related issues**: Keeping an eye out for these symptoms can identify and address issues at mealtime as soon as possible.
- **Avoid slapping someone on the back if they are coughing or choking**: If you slap someone on the back, the object may slide further down their throat and become more difficult to remove.
- **Always be ready to do the Heimlich maneuver**: This can save a life by removing a foreign item from a person's choking victim's airway.
- **If a choking person tries to leave the room, you should follow them**: In the event of an emergency, it is crucial that the person choking is accompanied at all times and that help is sought without delay.

Tips for Drinking Medicine

- **Do not panic**: When taking medication, it's best to do it with a cool and collected frame of mind, as anxiety or stress can interfere with swallowing.
- **Sit up straight**: Be sure you're sitting up straight so the medicine goes where it's supposed to, in your stomach, not your lungs.
- **Swallow one pill**: There is less of a chance of choking or aspiration if you take one pill at a time and can concentrate fully on the task.
- **Drink a glass of water**: Take medication capsules with a full glass of water to ease swallowing and prevent esophageal irritation. Pills are easier to swallow, less likely to cause esophageal blockage, and cause less irritation if taken with adequate liquid.

- **Don't drink too much water or other** fluids: Although it is recommended that pills be taken with a full glass of water, it is equally vital that you do not drink more than your body needs. If you want to be sure you're drinking enough water every day without causing any negative effects, follow the rules set forth by the government.
- **To make it easier to swallow pills, try applesauce**: Applesauce can help soften some medications' bitter taste and make them easier to swallow. Applesauce's consistency can make swallowing the pill easier and lessen the chance of choking.
- **Substitute easier-to-swallow pills with those approved by a doctor**: Liquid or dissolvable tablets are two examples of pharmaceutical delivery systems that might make taking medicine more convenient. Talk to your doctor or local pharmacy if you need help finding medication.
- **If you're allowed to, use a specific cup**: By regulating liquid flow and directing it to the rear of the mouth, spout, or angled cup, make pills simpler to swallow.
- **Medication is best taken first thing in the morning**: Prevent acid reflux and other digestive problems by spreading medicine intake throughout the day.
- **Stay upright after taking pills**: If you take medication, it's best to stay upright so that it doesn't become stuck in your esophagus or cause other digestive problems. After taking medication, sitting up straight for 30 minutes is best.

It is generally best to employ the same successful methods for swallowing liquids and solids (such as an effortful swallow and chin tuck, for example).

After Meal Tips

- **Stay upright for at least 30–45 minutes after eating**: Laying down raises the risk of aspiration pneumonia and choking on swallowed food or drink.
- **If possible, go for a brisk walk after eating**: This will aid digestion and keep food from getting stuck in your esophagus, lowering your chance of choking or aspirating.
- **Dentures, dental plaque, and teeth should be cleaned multiple times daily**: Regarding your health, nothing is more important than keeping up with your oral hygiene routine.
- **Rinse your mouth with an antibiotic solution as directed**: An infection-causing buildup of oral bacteria can be mitigated by regularly using an antibacterial mouthwash.

- **Moistening and lubricating the mouth with a swab can help in swallowing**: Using one on your lips, tongue, and cheeks is a good idea.
- **Sucking up accumulated saliva can help lower bacteria levels**: Infection-causing bacteria can thrive in a pool of saliva. The number of microorganisms in the mouth can be lowered by suctioning collected saliva.
- **Schedule biannual cleanings and checkups at the dentist**: This is a good way to keep your teeth and gums healthy and avoid infections and other complications.

Between Meals Tips

- **You should watch for signs of trouble** breathing: Any changes in the voice, breathing, wheezing, or chest pain should be taken seriously. Get checked out if you're experiencing anything suspicious.
- **Do the suggested exercises for swallowing**: Whenever a healthcare practitioner gives you specific instructions, perform activities that include breathing, coughing, and chewing. Perform these exercises regularly to strengthen your throat muscles and lower your chance of aspiration.
- **Maintain an active lifestyle**: Enhancing your balance, muscle strength, and posture to achieve a higher fitness level. Regular exercise helps boost health and lessen the likelihood of injury from slips, trips, and falls.
- **Stay sharp by challenging your brain**: You can use puzzles, board games, reading, and mentoring. Keeping your mind occupied is good for your health and sanity.
- **Raise the level of the top of the bed**: To avoid aspiration or reflux when sleeping, prop up your head with a wedge cushion or raise the mattress 30 degrees. It can be useful in preventing nocturnal choking and coughing.

CHAPTER 6

NUTRITION AND DYSPHAGIA:
REQUIREMENTS AND RECOMMENDATIONS

As you probably already know, taking in food and swallowing it should be a piece of cake. However, those who struggle with dysphagia may find this task more difficult. There are times when it's easier to swallow our pride than it is to chew and swallow our food.

Imagine you're at a posh dinner event, and your host gives you an exquisite dish that appears to be a work of art but is difficult to chew. You try to eat it with good manners, but as you swallow, you have the sensation of playing the game Chubby Bunny and trying to fit as many marshmallows as possible in your mouth. Feeling your cheeks swell like a squirrel as you attempt to shuffle the food around in your mouth but to no avail. You begin to worry, wondering if you must perform the Heimlich maneuver.

Have no fear; you are not alone. Those of us who struggle with dysphagia can relate. No need to worry, though; this chapter will cover all the bases regarding nutrition, including what you need to know and what you should eat, so you can eat delicious and healthy food without worrying about choking. So, unwind, and let's dig into the fascinating area of nutrition and dysphagia!

Everyone needs a well-rounded, nutritious diet to be in peak physical and mental condition. Getting enough nutrition, however, can be a major obstacle for people with dysphagia. Malnutrition and dehydration might occur if dysphagia is not treated.

Because of their difficulties swallowing, people with dysphagia are at an increased risk of malnutrition and dehydration, making it crucial to receive adequate nutrition. People with trouble swallowing often eat less because they shun certain meals or have difficulty swallowing others. Aspiration pneumonia, brought on by difficulty swallowing, can further damage nutrition and general health.

Fortunately, various approaches and methods can aid people with dysphagia in consuming the food they need to stay healthy. The health and well-being of people with dysphagia can be preserved and enhanced by giving them the nutrition they need as a top priority in treatment.

Dysphagia Patients' Dietary Requirements

People who have trouble swallowing have unique nutritional requirements. The inability to swallow normally due to dysphagia increases a person's risk of malnutrition and dehydration. Therefore, it is essential to learn about dysphagia and the specific nutritional requirements of those who have it.

Dysphagia patients sometimes struggle to consume enough food and nutrients to sustain their health. They may not eat enough, eat meals that are simple to consume but lack nutritious content, or avoid eating altogether due to their difficulties swallowing. A decrease in appetite and muscle strength are only two potential side effects.

Keeping water down is a struggle for those with dysphagia. They run the danger of dehydration because of the difficulty of consuming adequate fluids due to the difficulty of swallowing. Kidney damage, UTIs, and constipation are just a few of the many issues that can arise from dehydration.

Understanding the specific nutritional requirements of people with dysphagia is crucial for meeting these issues. People with dysphagia typically need more food and protein than those without the disorder if they want to keep the same weight and level of muscle mass. To avoid dehydration, they may need to drink additional fluids.

In other cases, though, this may not be as simple as boosting calorie and fluid intake. The foods and drinks should be well-tested for safety and simplicity of consumption. Some meals, for instance, might benefit from being pureed, mashed, or diced before being consumed. Aspiration can be avoided by increasing the viscosity of some liquids.

If a person has dysphagia, they must take extra measures to ensure they get the nutrients they need. Malnutrition can result in nutrient deficiencies such as a lack of vitamin D, calcium, or iron, which can contribute to developing other health issues.

Overall, those with dysphagia need a different method of feeding. Those with dysphagia can keep their health and quality of life on track if their specific nutritional demands are recognized and met.

Taking a Look at How Well Someone Is Eating

People with dysphagia need to eat well because they are more likely to become malnourished and dehydrated. People with dysphagia need regular checks on their nutritional status to make sure they are getting enough to eat. A nutritional assessment examines a person's diet, health, and medical background to determine their needed nutrients. There are several ways to figure out a person's nutritional state when they have dysphagia, such as:

Medical Background

A person's medical background can tell a lot about their eating well. This includes details about their current health, the medicines they take, and any surgeries they've had. It can also say what they like to eat and if they have any dietary limits.

Physical Checkup

A physical check can help determine if someone is malnourished or dehydrated by looking for things like wasting muscles, dry skin, or nails that break easily. It can also help determine if they have health problems that might hurt their nutrition.

Blood Tests

A person's nutritional levels, particularly those of the minerals iron, vitamin D, and calcium, can be determined through a blood test. They can also tell how well the person's kidneys and liver work, affecting how well they receive and use nutrients.

Dietary Assessment

A dietary review looks at a person's diet to see how much of certain important nutrients they get. One way to do this is with the help of a food journal or by merely asking the individual to recall what they ate at specific times. Assessing a person's diet and eating habits might help pinpoint potential problems.

To avoid more health problems, it's important to catch nutritional deficits early. Malnutrition can cause your immune system to weaken, your muscles to waste away, and other major health problems. It can also make you more likely to get an illness, heal slowly, or have other problems. So, finding nutritional deficits early can help keep these problems from happening and improve health.

Assessing nutritional state can help determine the best way to treat dysphagia and find out if there are any nutritional deficiencies. Feeding modifications may include making foods smoother or thinner, adding vitamins, or switching to enteral or parenteral feeding.

It is important to check the nutritional state of people with dysphagia to ensure they get enough food and avoid complications. By looking at a person's medical history, doing a physical check, getting blood tests, and evaluating their diet, doctors can find nutritional deficiencies and develop a treatment plan that fits their needs.

Modified Diets

People with dysphagia often need to change their meals to ensure they can swallow safely and effectively. Foods and drinks on a modified diet undergo modifications to improve their swallowability. People with dysphagia can use different modified meals, each with pros and cons.

The National Dysphagia Diet (NDD)

For those who have trouble swallowing, there is the National Dysphagia Diet (NDD), a standardized method for categorizing the consistency of food and beverages and texture. There are four stages: Pureed (Level 1), Mechanical Soft (Level 2), Advanced (Level 3), and Regular (Level 4). Dietary guidelines with defined tiers for food and drink consistencies are commonly employed in medical facilities to promote uniformity in dietary recommendations.

Chopped or Grinded Foods

Because of their difficulties chewing and swallowing, people with dysphagia are generally advised to eat foods that have been chopped or ground. These meals have been mashed, pureed, or otherwise processed into a smoother consistency to make them more manageable.

Thickening Liquids

People with dysphagia and trouble eating thin liquids often use thickened liquids. A thickening agent is added to liquids like water, juice, or milk to make them more manageable. You can choose between nectar, honey, or pudding consistency, depending on the person.

People with dysphagia can benefit from modified meals because they make swallowing safer and easier, but there are some things they can't do. Modified diets, for instance, may not be as tasty or gratifying as regular diets, leading to lower food intake and diminished enjoyment of eating. They can also take a lot of time and need special planning, which can be hard on the person taking care of the person.

Treatment of Dysphagia with Nutritional Supplements

People with dysphagia are more likely to be malnourished because they have trouble eating and swallowing. People with dysphagia are often told to take nutritional products to ensure they get all the necessary nutrients. There are many different nutritional pills, each with pros and cons.

Oral Nutritional Supplements

To enhance their diet, many people take nutritional supplements orally, which might be a liquid, a powder, or a pill. They come in different tastes and can be eaten independently or mixed into food and drinks.

Parenteral Nutrition

Direct intravenous feeding, or parenteral feeding, involves the administration of nutrients to a patient rather than to the digestive system. This is usually only done for people with serious dysphagia who can't take enteral nutrition.

Even though nutritional supplements can help people with dysphagia meet their nutritional goals, they also have some drawbacks. For example, some people may not be able to take nutritional vitamins by mouth well, especially if they have stomach problems. Infection and tube dislodgement are potential problems arising from enteral and parenteral nutrition.

Enteral Nutrition (EN)

Enteral nutrition is when a feeding tube sends food to the digestive system. This can be done with a nasogastric tube, put into the digestive tract through the nose, or with a gastrostomy tube, put straight into the stomach through surgery. Those with difficulty swallowing, such as those with dysphagia, may require enteral nutrition to ensure they get the necessary nutrients.

CHAPTER 7

100 RECIPES FOR DYSPHAGIA

Welcome, dysphagia-afflicted diners! Are you sick of the same old boring, mushy meals? Do you long for something with more flavor, excitement, and... swallowability? Don't worry, my fellow foodies; I've got the answer to all your foodie problems: One hundred healthy and tasty meals created with dysphagia in mind.

I can guess what you're thinking at this point. "Cooking? Me? Ha!" But have no fear, dear readers. These recipes are so easy that even your pet rock could prepare them. And let's be honest; your pet rock has likely been more helpful around the house than you have been lately.

You can use these recipes to demonstrate your kitchen mastery to your loved ones. You'll be famous (at least in the retirement community). You never know; maybe you'll become famous enough to host your food show. The era of Gordon Ramsay has ended; a new chef has arrived.

Not to jump the gun or anything. The first order of business is to prepare tasty and simple food to digest. And trust me when I say that your taste buds will be in heaven after trying these dishes. Our full menu includes hearty soups, delicious meals, and sweet treats.

The recipes here are organized by texture and consistency into several groups. Included in these categories are foods that are soft, pureed, based on the liquid, solids that have been altered, snacks, sweets, and drinks. All the dishes are excellent and healthy and created with people with dysphagia in mind.

Changing the texture and consistency of food can help some people with dysphagia eat more comfortably, but it's vital to remember that everyone is different in their requirements and capabilities. More severe cases of dysphagia may necessitate more drastic dietary adjustments, such as the exclusive use of pureed or liquid foods.

These 100 recipes are suitable for both experienced cooks and those who have never set foot in a kitchen before and will have you producing delicious meals in no time. Put an end to bland, mushy food once and for all since your taste buds are in for a treat. Thanks to these simple recipes, you can now eat tasty food even with dysphagia. Get a chef's apron (or your pet rock) and join me in the kitchen!

RECIPES FOR SOFT FOOD

RECIPE 1

Easy, Delicious, and Creamy Scrambled Eggs

This recipe for soft food is not only a healthy source of protein but can be readily customized by adding pureed veggies or cheese.

INGREDIENTS:

- 2 eggs
- 1 tbsp. milk
- 1 tbsp. butter
- Salt and pepper, to taste

DIRECTIONS:

1. Separate the eggs into a bowl, then add the milk, salt, and pepper, whisking to combine.
2. Begin by slowly melting the butter in a pan that won't stick.
3. After pouring the egg mixture into the pan, cook it over low heat, stirring it frequently with a spatula. Continue doing this until the eggs have reached the desired level of doneness.
4. Prepare and serve immediately.

RECIPE 2

Sweet Potato Mash

This soft food recipe is highly adaptable, making it possible to increase the nutritional value and enhance the flavor by adding pureed fruits and vegetables.

INGREDIENTS:

- 2 big sweet potatoes, peeled and chopped
- 2 tbsp. butter
- ¼ c. milk
- Salt and pepper, to taste

DIRECTIONS:

1. Sweet potatoes should be boiled in a kettle filled with water until they've become fork-tender.
2. Potatoes should be drained and returned to the saucepan after being drained.
3. Blend the potatoes using a potato masher or fork after adding the milk, butter, salt, and pepper.
4. Serve fresh.

RECIPE 3

Soup with Cream of Mushrooms

The benefit of making this recipe for soft food is that it is simple to chew and an excellent source of protein and vitamins.

INGREDIENTS:

- 1 tbsp. butter
- ½ c. minced onions
- ⅓ c. sliced mushrooms
- 1 tbsp. all-purpose flour
- ½ c. milk
- 1 c. chicken broth
- Salt and pepper, to taste

DIRECTIONS:

1. Butter should be melted in a pan over low to medium heat.
2. Cook the onions and mushrooms until they become tender and soft.
3. Mix in the flour while still cooking for another minute or two.
4. Slowly add the milk and chicken broth, whisking constantly.
5. Cook, stirring periodically, until the soup thickens, about 5-10 minutes.
6. Put in as much salt and pepper as you like.
7. Get ready to serve hot.

RECIPE 4

Fruit and Cottage Cheese Dish

One advantage of this soft food dish is that it can be readily customized to meet one's dietary needs by substituting different types of pureed fruit or seasonings like honey or cinnamon.

INGREDIENTS:

- ½ c. cottage cheese
- ½ c. diced fresh fruit (blueberries, bananas, or peaches, for example)

DIRECTIONS:

1. Scoop some cottage cheese into a serving dish.
2. Sprinkle some chopped fruit on top.
3. Refrigerate before serving.

RECIPE 5

Smoothie Fixins': Peanut Butter and Bananas

This soft food recipe is an ideal source of protein and can be modified readily and customized by adding mashed fruits or veggies.

INGREDIENTS:

- 1 perfectly ripe banana
- ½ c. milk
- 2 tbsp. creamy peanut butter
- 1 tbsp. honey

DIRECTIONS:

1. Cut the banana in half and peel it.
2. Combine the banana, peanut butter, milk, and honey using a blender until completely smooth.
3. Pour the contents into a glass.
4. Refrigerate before serving.

RECIPE 6

Creamy Carrot-Ginger Soup

The nutritional value of this soup is enhanced by the fact that it is suitable for persons with dysphagia who require a meal that is both soft and simple to swallow.

INGREDIENTS:

- 4 c. carrots, chopped
- 2 c. veggie broth
- 1 c. almond milk
- 1 tbsp. grated fresh ginger
- 1 tbsp. olive oil
- Salt and pepper, to taste

DIRECTIONS:

1. Olive oil should be heated over medium heat in a big saucepan.
2. Sauté the carrots and ginger for several minutes after adding the chopped vegetables.
3. Add the veggie broth and bring it to a boil.
4. Simmer until carrots are tender, reducing heat as needed.
5. Take it off the burner and set it down for a while to cool down.
6. Make sure the soup is smooth by blending or using an immersion blender.
7. Put the purée back into the pan and add the almond milk.
8. Warm up the soup, then season it with pepper and salt.

RECIPE 7

Creamy Mashed Potato

Mashed potatoes are an all-time favorite comfort food and a great source of carbs and other essential nutrients for those with difficulty swallowing, such as those with dysphagia.

INGREDIENTS:

- 3 medium-sized potatoes, diced after peeling
- 2 tbsp. butter
- ¼ c. milk
- Salt and pepper, to taste

DIRECTIONS:

1. The diced potatoes should be boiled in salted water till they are tender.
2. After draining the water, add the butter as well as the milk.
3. Make the potatoes smooth and creamy by mashing them using a potato masher or a fork.
4. Add pepper and salt to taste.

RECIPE 8

Baked Sweet Potato Mash

Not only is this dish simple to digest, but it is also high in fiber and a rich potassium and vitamin A source.

INGREDIENTS:

- 3 large sweet potatoes, peeled and sliced
- 2 tbsp. butter
- ¼ c. milk
- 1 tbsp. maple syrup
- Salt and cinnamon, to taste

DIRECTIONS:

1. Bring oven temperature up to 375 degrees Fahrenheit.
2. To soften the sweet potatoes, boil them in salted water after they are diced.
3. After draining the water, fill it with milk, butter, and maple syrup.
4. Turn the sweet potatoes into a silky and creamy purée by mashing them using a potato masher or a fork.
5. Salt and cinnamon can be added to taste as a seasoning.
6. Place the mashed sweet potatoes in a baking dish.
7. Put it in the oven for about 15 minutes, up to the point when the top is browned.

RECIPE 9

Creamy Risotto with Spinach and Mushrooms

The benefits of this spinach-filled risotto include its smooth texture, which makes it simple to consume, and its high concentration of iron and other vital vitamins and minerals.

INGREDIENTS:

- 1 c. Arborio rice
- 3 c. veggie broth
- 2 c. chopped spinach
- 1 c. thinly-sliced mushrooms
- ¼ c. Parmesan cheese gratings
- 2 tbsp. olive oil
- Salt and pepper, to taste

DIRECTIONS:

1. Heat the olive oil in a big saucepan over low to medium heat.
2. Put the rice in the pan and cook it for several minutes.
3. Add in some veggie broth and get it boiling.
4. Turn down the heat to a simmer and leave the rice to cook.
5. Chop some mushrooms and spinach and toss them in.
6. Spinach and mushrooms should be cooked for 5-10 minutes.
7. Turn off the heat and mix in the Parmesan.
8. Salt and pepper should be added according to your preference.

RECIPE 10

Greek Yogurt and Sweet Potato Mash

Because it contains a wealth of essential vitamins and minerals, this dish can greatly assist people struggling with dysphagia in meeting their dietary requirements. Those who have trouble swallowing will find that this dish, which features Greek yogurt as an important source of protein and the potato as a source of vitamin A, is an ideal option.

INGREDIENTS:

- Two sweet potatoes, roughly cut and skinned, of a medium size
- 2 tbsp. Greek yogurt
- 1 tbsp. unsalted butter
- Salt and pepper, to taste

DIRECTIONS:

1. To prepare the sweet potatoes, boil them until they are fork-tender.
2. After draining the water, mash the potatoes using a fork or a masher.
3. After adding the yogurt and unsalted butter, continue mashing the ingredients until thoroughly blended.
4. Salt and pepper should be added according to your preference.

RECIPE 11

Creamy Broccoli Soup

Individuals who struggle with dysphagia can benefit from the recipe's high fiber and calcium content because these nutrients are vital for their condition. Adding extra broth or milk to the creamy base can adjust the soup to the desired consistency.

INGREDIENTS:

- 2 c. frozen broccoli florets
- 1 c. chicken broth with less salt
- 1 c. whole milk
- 1 tbsp. unsalted butter
- Salt and pepper, to taste

DIRECTIONS:

1. Tenderize the broccoli by steaming it.
2. Blending steamed broccoli with low-sodium chicken broth and whole milk in a blender until smooth is the first step in making a broccoli soup.
3. Put everything in a pot and warm it up on the stove.
4. Stir in the unsalted butter until it has melted.
5. Salt and pepper should be added according to your preference.

RECIPE 12

Avocado Egg Salad

People with dysphagia can benefit greatly from this dish's high protein, healthy fat, and fiber content. The egg makes it soft and easy to swallow, while the avocado makes it creamy.

INGREDIENTS:

- 2 boiled eggs, peeled and sliced
- 1 small peeled and mashed avocado
- 1 tbsp. mayonnaise
- 1 tsp. mustard with a Dijon twist
- Salt and pepper, to taste

DIRECTIONS:

1. Chop the hard-boiled eggs and add them to the avocado, mayonnaise, Dijon mustard, and the rest of the ingredients in a bowl.
2. Put all the ingredients in a bowl and stir them together.
3. Put in as much salt and pepper as you like.

RECIPE 13

Risotto with Butternut Squash

The nutritional demands of people with dysphagia may be better met because of this dish's high fiber, vitamin, and mineral content. The risotto is easy to eat because of its smooth and creamy consistency.

INGREDIENTS:

- 1 c. Arborio rice
- 1 peeled and sliced mini butternut squash
- 3 c. chicken broth (low sodium)
- 1 tbsp. unsalted butter
- 1 small chopped onion
- ¼ c. Parmesan cheese gratings
- Salt and pepper, to taste

DIRECTIONS:

1. To make the chopped onion tender and translucent, sauté it in unsalted butter in a saucepan until it reaches the desired consistency.
2. After adding the Arborio rice, stir until it is completely covered.
3. Combine the butternut squash chunks with the rest of the ingredients.
4. The low-sodium chicken broth should be added in increments of ½ cup, stirred between additions, and absorbed before adding more.
5. Grated Parmesan cheese can be added when the butternut squash and rice are done cooking and stirred until melted.
6. Add pepper and salt to taste.

RECIPE 14

Banana Oatmeal

Oatmeal is a wonderful source of fiber, and when mixed with mashed banana, the texture becomes smooth and simple to swallow for those who struggle with dysphagia.

INGREDIENTS:

- 1 mashed ripe banana
- ½ c. instant oats
- 1 c. liquid, such as milk or water
- 1 tbsp. Honey
- ¼ tsp. cinnamon powder
- Salt, to taste

DIRECTIONS:

1. Mash the banana and add it to the oats, the liquid of your choice, cinnamon, honey, and salt in a pot.
2. Over medium heat, the mixture should be brought to a boil.
3. Turn the heat down and simmer for about seven minutes until the oats are cooked and the liquid thickens.
4. Serve hot.

RECIPE 15

Baked Oatmeal with Sweet Fruits

The high fiber content of these baked oats contributes to better bowel function. Dysphagia sufferers can benefit from the fruit's flavor and texture because it doesn't need a lot of chewing.

INGREDIENTS:

- 2 c. rolled oats
- ¼ c. brown sugar
- 1 tsp. baking powder
- 1 tsp. Cinnamon
- ¼ tsp. salt
- 2 c. milk
- 2 eggs
- 1 tsp. vanilla extract
- 1 c. any soft fruit, like berries or peaches

DIRECTIONS:

1. Warm a 9x9-inch baking dish in a preheated 375°F oven.
2. Combine the oats, baking soda, sugar, cinnamon, and salt in a large bowl.
3. In another bowl, combine the eggs, milk, and vanilla.
4. The wet ingredients should be added to the dry ones, and the two should be mixed.
5. Spread the fruit over the top of the mixture before pouring it into the baking dish.
6. If you want your oatmeal to be golden brown, bake it for 35-40 minutes.

RECIPE 16

Chicken and Rice with Cream Sauce

The benefit of this dish is that it offers a supply of soft and creamy carbohydrates and protein, making it suitable for people with dysphagia.

INGREDIENTS:

- 1 c. rice, cooked
- ⅓ c. chicken broth
- ⅓ c. heavy cream
- ⅓ shredded chicken (cooked)
- 1 tbsp. butter
- Salt and pepper, to taste

DIRECTIONS:

1. Bring the heavy cream and chicken broth to a low simmer in a low- to medium-powered saucepan for a few minutes.
2. Stir the chicken and cooked rice together in a saucepan.
3. Turn the heat low and season with salt, pepper, and butter. Melt the butter and mix everything by stirring.
4. Serve hot.

RECIPE 17

Creamy Cauliflower Puree

The benefit of using this cauliflower mash as an alternative to typical mashed potatoes is that it is easier for people with difficulty swallowing potatoes. It's a great way to get your daily vitamin C and fiber dose.

INGREDIENTS:

- 1 cauliflower head chopped down into florets
- 2 tbsp. butter
- ¼ c. full-fat cream
- Salt and pepper, to taste

DIRECTIONS:

1. Cauliflower should be steamed or boiled until it is quite tender.
2. After it has been drained, place the cauliflower, heavy cream, and butter in a blender or food processor.
3. Make a smooth puree with a blender.
4. Depending on your taste, add salt and pepper.

RECIPE 18

Salmon with Pureed Vegetables

This salmon and veggie puree is a wonderful way to get your daily dose of protein, omega-3 fats, and vitamins. The pureed texture and mild consistency make it suitable for people with dysphagia.

INGREDIENTS:

- 1 lb. salmon (without the skin)
- 2 c. carrots, zucchini, and celery, diced
- 1 c. chicken broth
- 1 tbsp. olive oil
- Pepper and salt, to taste

DIRECTIONS:

1. The oven needs to be preheated at 350 degrees Fahrenheit.
2. Combine the salmon and veggies in a baking dish and sprinkle with olive oil. Add salt and pepper to taste.
3. The chicken broth should be poured on top.
4. Put the salmon in the oven and bake for 20-25 minutes.
5. Prepare a smooth puree by blending the fish and veggies.

RECIPE 19

Egg and Avocado Salad

The avocado and eggs in this salad make for a softer and creamier version of the classic egg salad. It's a great way to get protein, vitamins, and healthy fats.

INGREDIENTS:

- 2 sliced hard-boiled eggs
- 1 ripe avocado, mashed
- 1 tbsp. plain Greek yogurt
- 1 tbsp. finely minced chives
- Pepper and salt, to taste

DIRECTIONS:

1. Combine the diced eggs, smashed chives, mashed avocado, and Greek yogurt in a bowl and stir thoroughly.
2. Depending on your taste, add salt and pepper.

RECIPE 20

Creamy Rice Made with Cauliflower

The benefit of this tasty and smooth cauliflower rice is that people with dysphagia can easily swallow it and have trouble eating other types of rice.

INGREDIENTS:

- 1 c. riced cauliflower
- 1 tbsp. olive oil
- 1 small onion, diced
- 2 minced garlic cloves
- 1 c. broth, either chicken or vegetable
- ½ c. full-fat cream
- Salt and pepper, to taste

DIRECTIONS:

1. Olive oil should be heated in a big pan over medium heat.
2. Toss in some garlic and onions and cook them down until they are transparent.
3. Bring the stock and cauliflower rice to a boil.
4. Turn the heat down and boil the cauliflower for a few minutes.
5. Take off the stove and combine everything in a blender.
6. Blend in the whole milk and adjust the seasoning with the pepper and salt.

RECIPES FOR PUREED FOODS

RECIPE 21

Creamy Cauliflower Puree

This pureed cauliflower meal is an excellent option for those with dysphagia because it contains vegetables with a smooth texture and is easy to swallow.

INGREDIENTS:

- Florets from one cauliflower head
- ¼ c. full-fat cream
- 2 tbsp. butter
- Salt and pepper, to taste

DIRECTIONS:

1. The cauliflower florets need around 10 minutes of steaming time to become soft.
2. Blend or process the steamed cauliflower with the cream and butter until smooth.
3. Put in as much salt and pepper as you like.

RECIPE 22

Pureed Chicken and Rice

This chicken and rice meal has the added benefit of being pureed, making the protein and carbohydrates easier to consume.

INGREDIENTS:

- 1 c. cooked white rice
- 1 c. chopped chicken
- ½ c. chicken broth
- ¼ c. sour cream
- Salt and pepper, to taste

DIRECTIONS:

1. Blend cooked rice with chicken broth, sour cream, and chopped chicken in a blender or food processor.
2. Add pepper and salt to taste.

RECIPE 23

Pureed Sweet Potatoes

The pureed form of sweet potatoes is a delightful and easy method to add these nutritious tubers to a diet for those with dysphagia.

INGREDIENTS:

- 2 big, peeled, and sliced sweet potatoes
- ¼ c. Milk
- 2 tbsp. butter
- 1 tbsp. honey
- ½ tsp. ground cinnamon
- Salt, to taste

DIRECTIONS:

1. Sweet potato chunks should be boiled in salted water for 15-20 minutes or until fork-tender.
2. After draining the sweet potatoes, place them in a blender with butter, milk, cinnamon, and honey.
3. Blend until smooth.

RECIPE 24

Apple Puree

Incorporating fruit into a diet restricted by dysphagia can be challenging, but apple sauce is a timeless pureed food that makes it easy and delicious.

INGREDIENTS:

- 4 medium-sized apples, peeled and diced
- ¼ c. water
- 1 tbsp. Lemon juice
- ¼ tsp. Ground cinnamon

DIRECTIONS:

1. In a pot, boil water, chopped apples, cinnamon, and lemon juice, for 15-20 minutes.
2. Cool slightly off the stove before mixing in a blender or food processor.

RECIPE 25

Pureed Tuna and Veggies

The pureed tuna and veggies in this recipe offer the health benefits of protein and vegetables while being incredibly palatable.

INGREDIENTS:

- 1 drained can of tuna
- ½ c. chopped cooked carrots
- ½ c. chopped cooked green beans
- ¼ c. mayonnaise
- ¼ c. sour cream
- Salt and pepper, to taste

DIRECTIONS:

1. Blend or process the canned tuna, green beans, carrots, sour cream, and mayonnaise until smooth.
2. Add pepper and salt to taste.

RECIPE 26

Pureed Carrot Soup

This pureed carrot soup is a healthy and full option for people with trouble swallowing because of its high vitamin A and fiber content.

INGREDIENTS:

- 1 lb. peeled and diced carrots
- 2 c. chicken or vegetable broth
- 1 small onion, diced
- 1 c. milk or cream
- Salt and pepper, to taste

DIRECTIONS:

1. Carrots and onion should be cooked in a big saucepan until tender in the broth.
2. The cooked vegetables should be blended until smooth.
3. Pour milk or cream into the pot with the pureed mixture until it reaches the desired consistency.
4. Put in as much salt and pepper as you like.

RECIPE 27

Pureed Chicken and Rice

This meal is beneficial since it is high in protein and can be readily customized by adding new herbs and spices.

INGREDIENTS:

- 1 lb. chicken breasts, skinless and boneless
- 1 c. cooked white rice
- 2 c. chicken stock
- Pepper and salt, to taste.

DIRECTIONS:

1. To ensure the chicken is cooked through and soft, simmer it in chicken broth.
2. The chicken and broth should be blended until completely smooth.
3. Blend in the cooked rice until everything is well-combined.
4. Add pepper and salt to taste.

RECIPE 28

Pureed Sweet Potato

This has many health benefits, including being simple to swallow for people with dysphagia due to its smooth consistency and high levels of beta-carotene and vitamin C.

INGREDIENTS:

- 2 medium-sized sweet potatoes, diced and peeled
- 1 c. broth, either chicken or vegetable
- ½ g. butter
- Pepper and salt as per taste preference

DIRECTIONS:

1. Tenderize the sweet potatoes by cooking them in the broth.
2. Combine cooked sweet potatoes with broth and butter in a blender to make a smooth puree.
3. Put in as much salt and pepper as you like.

RECIPE 29

Pureed Turkey and Gravy

This dish, which consists of pureed turkey and gravy, is advantageous since it is high in protein and may be supplemented with other pureed foods, such as vegetables or mashed potatoes, to provide a full meal.

INGREDIENTS:

- 1 lb. cooked and shredded turkey breast
- 1 c. chicken or turkey broth
- ½ c. milk or cream
- Salt and pepper, to taste

DIRECTIONS:

1. Warm the turkey and broth in a large pot until the turkey is completely cooked.
2. You can make a smooth turkey and broth puree by using a blender.
3. Mix in the cream or milk with the remaining ingredients in the blender.
4. Put in as much salt and pepper as you like.

RECIPE 30

Banana and Yogurt Puree

The banana and yogurt puree is a fantastic option for people with trouble swallowing because of its high potassium and probiotic content.

INGREDIENTS:

- 2 ripe bananas
- 1 c. plain Greek yogurt
- ½ c. milk
- 1 tsp. Honey (Optional)

DIRECTIONS:

1. Blend the bananas, milk, yogurt, and honey until completely smooth.
2. If required, add more milk or yogurt to achieve the desired consistency.

RECIPE 31

Pureed Chicken and Vegetable Casserole

This dish can be prepared in advance and heated up when needed for a complete and easily digested dinner.

INGREDIENTS:

- 1 lb. chicken breasts, skinless and boneless
- 2 c. mixed veggies (broccoli, cauliflower, green peppers, etc.)
- ½ c. chicken or vegetable broth
- 1 tbsp. olive oil
- Pepper and salt, to taste

DIRECTIONS:

1. Set oven temperature to 375 degrees Fahrenheit.
2. Sprinkle some salt and pepper on the chicken breasts.
3. In a large skillet, warm the olive oil over moderate heat.
4. Prepare the chicken by adding it to the pan and browning it on both sides.
5. Take the chicken out of the skillet.
6. Cook the vegetables in a skillet until they are fork-tender.
7. Pour in the broth and mix thoroughly.
8. Put the chicken and veggies in a blender and blend until completely smooth.
9. Put the ingredients in a casserole dish and bake at 350 degrees for 20 to 25 minutes.

RECIPE 32

A Rich and Creamy Mushroom Puree

This puree is beneficial since it is high in protein and has a smooth texture, making it suitable for those with difficulty swallowing.

INGREDIENTS:

- 2 c. sliced mushrooms
- ½ c. full-fat cream
- ¼ c. chicken or vegetable broth
- 1 tbsp. butter
- Salt and pepper according to taste.

DIRECTIONS:

1. The butter needs to be melted over medium heat in a big skillet.
2. Cook the mushrooms in the butter until they are soft.
3. Cook for 5-10 minutes at a low simmer after adding the broth.
4. Take it off the stove and let it cool.
5. Blend the mushrooms until they are completely smooth.
6. Put everything back in the pan and add the heavy cream.
7. Warm the ingredients together over low heat.
8. Salt and pepper can be added according to personal preference.

RECIPE 33

Fruit Puree with Greek Yogurt

Dysphagia patients can add diversity to their diets with this Greek yogurt and fruit puree. Vitamins, antioxidants, and protein can all be found in plenty in the blend.

INGREDIENTS:

- 1 c. Greek yogurt
- 1 c. mixed berries (blueberries, strawberries, raspberries, etc.)
- ¼ c. honey
- 1 tsp. vanilla extract

DIRECTIONS:

1. Blend the Greek yogurt, fruit, honey, and vanilla extract.
2. Mix until a smooth consistency is reached.
3. Make sure it's cold before serving.

RECIPE 34

Carrot-Ginger Puree

This pureed soup made from carrots and ginger is an excellent source of vitamins A and C and provides a little heat to the meal for people with difficulty swallowing.

INGREDIENTS:

- 4 big carrots, peeled and sliced
- 1 onion, chopped
- 1-inch grated ginger
- 2 c. chicken or vegetable broth
- ½ c. full-fat cream
- Salt and pepper, to taste

DIRECTIONS:

1. To make this soup, put the onion, carrots, chicken or vegetable broth, and ginger in a large pot and stir to mix.
2. The carrots should be cooked at a simmering temperature after 20-25 minutes from when the mixture is brought to a boil.
3. Smooth up any lumps with either a mixer or an immersion blender.
4. Blend in the whole milk and adjust the seasoning with salt and pepper.

RECIPE 35

Creamy Butternut Squash Soup

This dysphagia-friendly soup has vitamin A, fiber, and potassium.

INGREDIENTS:

- 1 medium butternut squash, peeled, seeded, and chopped
- 1 small onion, diced
- 2 minced garlic cloves
- 2 c. chicken broth
- 1 c. full-fat cream
- ¼ tsp. nutmeg
- Salt and pepper, to taste

DIRECTIONS:

1. Put the butternut squash, garlic, onion, and chicken broth in a large pot and stir to mix. Squash should be very soft after boiling for 20–25 minutes at low heat.
2. Smooth up any lumps with either a mixer or an immersion blender.
3. Pureed ingredients should be returned to the kettle and combined with nutmeg and heavy cream. Bring to a boil, then add salt & pepper to taste when it's been heated through.

RECIPE 36

Greek Yogurt & Berry Smoothie

This smoothie's Greek yogurt, milk, and assorted berries produce a healthy dose of protein, calcium, and antioxidants. People with dysphagia can like it because it tastes good and is simple to swallow.

INGREDIENTS:

- 1 c. Greek yogurt
- ½ c. mixed berries
- ½ c. milk
- 1 ½ g. honey

DIRECTIONS:

1. Blend everything until it's nice and creamy.
2. The mixture should be poured into a glass, and it should be served straight away.

RECIPE 37

Creamy Broccoli Puree with Cheese

Dysphagia patients may easily swallow this puree containing calcium and fiber from broccoli and cheese.

INGREDIENTS:

- 2 c. steamed broccoli florets
- ½ c. cream cheese
- ¼ c. grated Parmesan cheese
- ¼ c. milk
- Salt and pepper, to taste

DIRECTIONS:

1. Put the broccoli that has been steamed, the cream cheese, the Parmesan cheese, and the milk into a blender and mix until smooth.
2. Whisk the puree frequently as it heats in a pot over low heat.
3. Depending on your taste, add salt and pepper.

RECIPE 38

Rich Vanilla Pudding

Delicious pudding is a nutritious choice for persons with dysphagia because it is made with milk and eggs, which are high in protein.

INGREDIENTS:

- 2 c. regular milk
- ⅓ c. white sugar
- ¼ c. cornstarch
- 2 whole eggs
- 2 tsp. Vanilla extract.

DIRECTIONS:

1. Using a medium saucepan, thoroughly combine the milk, cornstarch, and sugar by whisking the ingredients together.
2. Add the egg yolks and whisk until fully combined.
3. Whisk the mixture continually as it cooks over medium heat to ensure a smooth consistency, and bring it to a boil.
4. Turn off the heat and add the vanilla essence to the pudding.
5. Spoon the pudding into serving bowls and place it in the fridge to solidify.

RECIPES FOR LIQUID FOOD

RECIPE 39

Creamy Potato Soup

This soup has a smooth, creamy consistency that is easy on the throat.

INGREDIENTS:

- 1 c. potato mash
- 1 c. chicken broth
- ½ c. full-fat cream
- 1 tbsp. butter
- Pepper and salt, to taste

DIRECTIONS:

1. Stir in chicken broth to the mashed potatoes and bring to a boil.
2. Toss in some butter and heavy cream and lower the heat to medium. Mix thoroughly by stirring.
3. Add pepper and salt to taste.
4. The soup can be blended smoothly using an immersion blender.
5. Prepare and serve hot.

RECIPE 40

Strawberry and Banana

This smoothie has several health benefits, including refreshing and healthy liquid food.

INGREDIENTS:

- 1 banana
- 1 c. frozen strawberries
- 1 c. milk
- ½ c. vanilla yogurt
- 1 tbsp. Honey

DIRECTIONS:

1. Put everything in a blender.
2. Make a smooth paste by blending.
3. Serve cold.

RECIPE 41

Tomato Basil Soup

The soup has a pleasant flavor and is easy to digest because of its liquid form.

INGREDIENTS:

- 1 can tomato soup
- ½ c. full-fat cream
- 1 tbsp. butter
- 1 tbsp. fresh chopped basil
- Salt and pepper, to taste

DIRECTIONS:

1. Bring the tomato soup to a simmer over low to medium heat.
2. Combine basil, butter, and heavy cream, and serve. Mix thoroughly by stirring.
3. Prepare to taste with salt and pepper.
4. Use an immersion blender to puree the soup.
5. Prepare and serve hot.

RECIPE 42

Carrot Ginger Soup

This soup has the added benefit of being a healthful and easy-to-swallow liquid food. The anti-inflammatory properties of ginger may alleviate discomfort experienced when trying to swallow.

INGREDIENTS:

- 1 lb. carrots, chopped
- 1 tbsp. fresh ginger, minced
- 1 tbsp. butter
- 1 c. chicken broth
- Salt and pepper, to taste

DIRECTIONS:

1. In a saucepan, melt the butter over medium heat.
2. Put in some ginger and carrots. Carrots should be soft after cooking.
3. Put in some chicken broth and get it boiling.
4. Turn the heat down and let the food simmer for ten to fifteen minutes.
5. Use an immersion blender to puree the soup.
6. Depending on your taste, add salt and pepper.
7. Prepare and serve hot.

RECIPE 43

Creamy Vegetable Soup

This soup is loaded with healthy veggies and can be readily customized to suit individual tastes. The texture is soft and creamy, making it suitable for those with dysphagia.

INGREDIENTS:

- 1 c. steamed or boiled greens, root vegetables, or broccoli
- 1 c. broth, either chicken or vegetable
- ½ c. full-fat cream
- 1 tbsp. unsalted butter
- Salt and pepper, to taste

DIRECTIONS:

1. Combine the cooked veggies with the chicken or vegetable broth in a blender.
2. Turn on a pot to medium heat and bring the puree to a simmer.
3. Mix the unsalted butter and heavy cream until everything is combined.
4. Add pepper and salt to taste.
5. Keep warm and serve.

RECIPE 44

Smoothie with Blueberries

The antioxidant-rich blueberries in this smoothie are an excellent addition to the diets of those who have difficulty swallowing. Greek yogurt and almond milk produce a healthy dose of calcium and protein, while honey and vanilla flavors lend a pleasant taste.

INGREDIENTS:

- 1 c. blueberries, fresh or frozen
- ½ c. plain Greek yogurt
- ½ c. unsweetened almond milk
- 1 tbsp. Honey
- ½ tsp. vanilla essence

DIRECTIONS:

1. Put everything in a blender and mix it up until it's completely smooth.
2. Depending on how thick you like it, add additional almond milk.
3. Make sure to serve it cold.

RECIPE 45

Broccoli Cheese Soup

This soup not only adds healthy nutrients like fiber and calcium but also makes it easy to consume for those who struggle with swallowing, as the soup is very smooth and creamy.

INGREDIENTS:

- 1 c. chicken or vegetarian broth
- ½ c. shredded cheddar cheese
- 2 c. steamed broccoli
- ¼ c. full-fat cream
- 1 tbsp. unsalted butter
- Salt and pepper, to taste

DIRECTIONS:

1. Using a blender, make a smooth purée of the cooked broccoli by combining it with chicken or vegetable broth.
2. Turn on a pot to medium heat and bring the puree to a simmer.
3. Stir in the heavy cream, unsalted butter, and shredded cheddar cheese until evenly mixed.
4. Depending on your taste, add salt and pepper.
5. Serve hot.

RECIPE 46

Banana Pudding

The bananas in this pudding are an excellent source of potassium, and the pudding also contains protein and calcium, thanks to the mix of almond milk, Greek yogurt, and heavy cream. Honey and vanilla essence sweeten things up without masking the banana's inherent flavor.

INGREDIENTS:

- 2 ripe bananas
- ½ c. plain Greek yogurt
- ½ c. unsweetened almond milk
- ¼ c. full-fat cream
- 1 ½ g. honey
- ½ tsp. vanilla extract

DIRECTIONS:

1. Blend all the ingredients in a blender until they are completely combined.
2. Add more almond milk to achieve the desired consistency.
3. Make sure to serve the dish cold.

RECIPE 47

The Broccoli Cheddar Soup

Broccoli cheddar soup is a nutritious and comforting option for dysphagia patients since it contains vitamin C, fiber, and K.

INGREDIENTS:

- 6 c. low-sodium chicken broth
- 1 c. chopped broccoli
- 1 c. shredded cheddar cheese
- ½ c. full-fat cream
- 1 ½ g. butter
- Salt and pepper to taste.

DIRECTIONS:

1. Put the broccoli florets and chicken broth in a big pot.
2. The broccoli should be tender after 20-25 minutes of simmering the soup at low heat.
3. Take the saucepan off the stove and set it aside to cool.
4. The soup should be blended or blended with an immersion blender until smooth.
5. Put the soup back in the pot and mix the heavy cream, butter, and cheddar cheese.
6. The soup should be reheated over low heat with periodic stirring.
7. Salt and pepper can be added according to personal preference.

RECIPE 48

Blueberry Oatmeal

This blueberry oatmeal smoothie is loaded with healthy nutrients like antioxidants, fiber, and protein, making it an excellent choice for those with dysphagia who require a liquid meal.

INGREDIENTS:

- 1 c. frozen blueberries
- ½ c. rolled oats
- ½ c. vanilla yogurt
- 1 c. unsweetened almond milk
- 1 tbsp. Honey (optional)

DIRECTIONS:

1. Get a blender going and throw in some frozen blueberries, rolled oats, vanilla yogurt, and almond milk.
2. Mix until the mixture is velvety.
3. Sweeten with honey if you like.
4. Enjoy best when served cold.

RECIPE 49

Chicken Noodle Soup

Dysphagia patients can enjoy this high-protein, vegetable-packed chicken noodle soup.

INGREDIENTS:

- 1 lb. skinless, boneless chicken breasts
- 4 c. chicken broth
- 2 c. water
- 2 medium carrots
- 2 celery stalks
- 1 small onion
- 2 garlic cloves, minced
- 2 c. egg noodles
- Salt and pepper, to taste

DIRECTIONS:

1. Add all the ingredients (chicken, broth, water, veggies, onion, garlic, etc.) into a big saucepan and boil.
2. The chicken should be cooked thoroughly after the mixture has been brought to a boil and then reduced to a simmer.
3. Take the chicken out of the cooking liquid and shred it using two forks.
4. Put the noodles back in the pan with the shredded chicken.
5. Leave on low heat until the noodles are cooked.
6. Prepare to taste with salt and pepper.
7. Enjoy while hot!

RECIPE 50

Butternut Squash Soup

Besides being high in beneficial vitamins and minerals, this soup also has healthy fats from the coconut milk, which aids in feeling full and giving the soup a richer texture.

INGREDIENTS:

- 1 squash, butternut, peeled and diced
- 1 c. minced onion
- 2 c. chicken or veggie broth
- 1 c. coconut milk
- 1 tsp. ground ginger
- Salt and pepper, to taste

DIRECTIONS:

1. Sauté the onion in a large saucepan until it is soft.
2. Throw in some butternut squash chunks and some broth, and get the pot boiling.
3. Turn the heat down, cover, and cook the squash until soft.
4. Use a blender to liquefy the soup completely.
5. Blend in some coconut milk, some ginger, some salt, and some pepper.

RECIPE 51

Broccoli-Cheddar Soup

The pureed texture makes it suitable for dysphagia patients because it is easy to swallow while still providing a healthy dose of calcium and fiber from the broccoli and cheddar cheese.

INGREDIENTS:

- 1 lb. broccoli flowers
- 1 sliced onion
- 2 c. chicken or veggie broth
- 1 c. shredded cheddar cheese
- Salt and pepper, to taste

DIRECTIONS:

1. Sauté the onion in a large saucepan until it is soft.
2. Toss in some broccoli and some broth and get them boiling.
3. Turn the heat down, cover, and boil the broccoli for a few minutes.
4. Blend the soup until it is completely smooth.
5. Blend in some grated cheddar cheese until it is completely blended.
6. Salt and pepper can be added according to personal preference.

RECIPE 52

Creamy Tomato Soup

Both advantages are the lycopene in the tomatoes and the smoothness of the soup's texture from the heavy cream.

INGREDIENTS:

- 2 28-ounce cans of tomato paste
- 1 small onion, diced
- 1 minced clove of garlic
- 2 c. chicken or veggie broth
- 1 c. full-fat cream
- Salt and pepper, to taste

DIRECTIONS:

1. Sauté the onion and garlic in a large pot until soft.
2. Toss in some crushed tomatoes and broth, then turn the heat high.
3. Bring to a simmer, cover, and cook for 15 to 20 minutes.
4. You can use a blender to make a smooth puree of the soup.
5. Combine the heavy cream with the rest of the ingredients.
6. Put in as much salt and pepper as you like.

RECIPE 53

Creamy Broccoli Soup

This soup's nutritional value and manageability make it a good choice for those with dysphagia who have trouble chewing and swallowing solid foods.

INGREDIENTS:

- 2 c. finely chopped broccoli
- 1 c. vegetable broth
- 1 c. full-fat milk
- 1 tbsp. butter
- Pepper and salt, to taste.

DIRECTIONS:

1. Simmer the broccoli in the vegetable broth for 10 minutes after bringing it to a boil.
2. Blend the cooked broccoli and broth until smooth, then set aside.
3. In a pot, melt the butter over low heat and add the heavy cream.
4. Stir the pureed broccoli and broth together in a large pot.
5. Put in as much salt and pepper as you like.

RECIPES FOR SOLID FOOD

RECIPE 54

Gravy-Coated Meatballs

People with dysphagia can benefit from eating meatballs in gravy because they are a tasty and gentle way to get protein.

INGREDIENTS:

- 1 lb. ground meat, beef or turkey
- ½ c. breadcrumbs
- ¼ c. milk
- ¼ c. grated parmesan
- 1 egg
- ½ tsp. Salt
- ¼ tsp. black pepper
- 2 c. chicken or beef broth
- 2 tbsp. cornstarch

DIRECTIONS:

1. To bake successfully, heat the oven to 375 degrees Fahrenheit.
2. Combine the ground meat, milk, bread crumbs, egg, parmesan cheese, salt, and pepper in a big dish and mix well.
3. Roll the minced meat into 1-inch balls.
4. Ensure the meatballs are properly cooked by baking them for 20-25 minutes.
5. The broth should be heated in a separate pot over medium heat.
6. Mix ¼ cup of cold water and cornstarch in a small dish until smooth.
7. While stirring constantly, gradually add the cornstarch mixture to the broth.
8. Serve the meatballs with the gravy poured over them.

RECIPE 55

Ground Turkey Meatloaf

Those who have trouble chewing or swallowing whole meats will benefit greatly from this adapted meatloaf because it is tender and simple to chew and swallow.

INGREDIENTS:

- ½ c. breadcrumbs
- 1 lb. ground turkey
- ¼ c. milk
- 1 egg, whisked
- ¼ c. chopped onion
- ¼ c. chopped green pepper
- ¼ c. chopped celery
- Salt and pepper, to taste

DIRECTIONS:

1. Start by setting your oven temperature to 350 degrees Fahrenheit.
2. Mix the ground turkey, milk, breadcrumbs, onion, egg, celery, and green pepper in a big bowl to make the meatballs.
3. Put in as much salt and pepper as you like.
4. Put the batter into a loaf pan that has been oiled and bake for 45-50 minutes.
5. Cool the meatloaf for a few minutes before slicing it into manageable pieces.

RECIPE 56

Avocado Scrambled Eggs

This recipe improves traditional scrambled eggs' nutritional value and soft texture, making them more accessible to those with dysphagia.

INGREDIENTS:

- 2 eggs
- Quarter ripe avocado, mashed
- 1 tbsp. butter
- Salt and pepper, to taste

DIRECTIONS:

1. In a basin, beat the eggs together.
2. Butter should be heated over medium heat in a nonstick skillet.
3. The eggs should be added and gently stirred until they reach the desired doneness.
4. Turn off the heat and add the mashed avocado to the skillet.
5. Put in as much salt and pepper as you like.

RECIPE 57

Roasted Vegetable Puree

This dish is a healthier option than eating raw veggies because it is cooked until it is soft and simple to swallow.

INGREDIENTS:

- 2 c. chopped vegetables (such as broccoli, cauliflower, and zucchini)
- 2 tbsp. olive oil
- Salt and pepper, to taste

DIRECTIONS:

1. Get the oven up to temperature, preferably 400 degrees Fahrenheit.
2. Sprinkle salt and pepper on the chopped vegetables and toss them in olive oil.
3. Roast the vegetables for 25-30 minutes, stirring once, until tender.
4. Cool down the vegetables slightly before blending them in a blender.
5. Serve hot.

RECIPE 58

Chicken and Rice Casserole

This recipe makes a well-balanced meal with grains from rice and protein from the chicken. For people who have trouble swallowing, this help changes the taste.

INGREDIENTS:

- 1 c. cooked rice
- ½ c. cooked, shredded chicken breast
- ½ c. carrot puree
- ¼ tsp. garlic powder
- ½ c. chicken broth
- Salt and pepper, to taste

DIRECTIONS:

1. Start by setting your oven temperature to 350 degrees Fahrenheit.
2. Add the rice, carrot puree, chicken, garlic powder, chicken broth, salt, and pepper to a bowl.
3. Place the contents of the bowl into a casserole dish, then bake for 20-25 minutes or until warmed through.
4. Set aside to cool before serving.

RECIPE 59

Black Bean and Sweet Potato Bowl

This dish is delicious and healthy, but it's also easy to digest for people with dysphagia.

INGREDIENTS:

- 1 c. sweet potato puree
- ½ c. black bean puree
- ¼ c. salsa
- ¼ c. sour cream
- A pinch of cumin
- Salt and pepper, to taste

DIRECTIONS:

1. Blend the sweet potato and black beans in a food processor until they form a smooth paste.
2. Add the sour cream, cumin, salsa, salt, and pepper.
3. Combine thoroughly, then dish out.

RECIPE 60

Beef Stroganoff

In addition to providing protein from the beef, this dish is flavorful and filling because of the onions, pureed mushrooms, and carrots, which also benefit those with dysphagia by changing the dish's texture.

INGREDIENTS:

- 1 c. cooked beef puree
- ½ c. mushroom puree
- ½ c. onion puree
- ½ c. sour cream
- ½ c. beef broth
- 1 tsp. Worcestershire sauce
- Salt and pepper, to taste

DIRECTIONS:

1. Mix the ground beef, onions, mushrooms, broth, sour cream, salt, Worcestershire sauce, and pepper in a pan.
2. Stir occasionally while heating over medium heat.
3. Carrots or mashed potatoes can be used as a topping for this dish.

RECIPE 61

Chicken with Sweet Potato Mash

This dish's chicken and sweet potato mash makes for a nutritious, palatable, easy-to-digest supper.

INGREDIENTS:

- 1 c. shredded cooked chicken breast
- ½ c. mashed sweet potato
- ½ c. chicken broth
- Pepper and salt, to taste

DIRECTIONS:

1. Mix the mashed sweet potato, shredded chicken, and broth in a large bowl. Put in as much salt and pepper as you like.
2. Mash the ingredients with a fork or a potato masher until they're completely combined and uniform in texture.
3. Serve hot.

RECIPE 62

Chicken and Rice Casserole

The chicken and rice in this recipe and the mashed veggies make for a tasty and manageable casserole.

INGREDIENTS:

- 1 c. shredded chicken breasts cooked
- ½ c. rice
- 1 c. chicken broth
- ¼ c. carrots, boiled and mashed
- ¼ c. mashed cooked green beans
- Pepper and salt, as desired

DIRECTIONS:

1. To bake successfully, heat the oven to 375 degrees Fahrenheit.
2. Mix the mashed veggies with the chicken, rice, and broth in a large bowl. Taste and adjust salt and pepper.
3. Put the ingredients in a casserole and bake at 350° for 20–25 minutes.
4. Serve at room temperature.

RECIPE 63

Salad with Shredded Chicken

This dish's shredded chicken and mashed veggies make for an easy-to-digest and healthy main dish.

INGREDIENTS:

- 1 c. shredded chicken breasts cooked
- ½ c. carrot puree
- ½ c. mashed green beans
- 1 tbsp. mayo
- Pepper and salt, as desired

DIRECTIONS:

1. Combine the carrots, chicken, and green beans in a bowl and stir well.
2. Blend in the mayonnaise. Taste and adjust salt and pepper.
3. Ideally, the dish would be served cold.

RECIPE 64

Red Sauce Meatballs

The tomato sauce adds more moisture to make these meatballs easier to swallow and soft.

INGREDIENTS:

- 1 lb. ground meat
- ½ c. breadcrumbs
- ¼ c. milk
- ¼ c. grated Parmesan
- 1 egg
- ¼ c. parsley and onion, each diced
- 1 tsp. garlic powder
- Pepper and salt, as desired
- 1 jar (24 oz.) Salsa tomato

DIRECTIONS:

1. Turn the oven temperature up to 375 degrees Fahrenheit.
2. Mix the bread crumbs, ground beef, Parmesan cheese, milk, parsley, egg, garlic powder, onion, salt, and pepper in a bowl. Combine all of the ingredients.
3. Make meatballs from the mixture and set them on a baking sheet.
4. Put the meatballs in the oven and bake for 15-20 minutes.
5. Tomato sauce should be heated over medium heat in a pot. Simmer the sauce for 5-10 minutes before adding the prepared meatballs.
6. Eat the meatballs with the sauce.

RECIPE 65

Slow-Cooked Shredded Chicken

Chicken cooked in a slow cooker is extremely soft and simple to chew and swallow. The chicken is more pleasant to eat after being shredded.

INGREDIENTS:

- 2 lb. chicken breasts without the bones or skin
- 1 c. barbeque sauce
- ¼ c. chicken broth
- 1 tsp. dried garlic
- Salt and pepper, as desired

DIRECTIONS:

1. Put chicken breasts in the slow cooker and turn it on low.
2. Mix the chicken broth, garlic powder, BBQ sauce, salt, and pepper in a bowl. Combine all of the ingredients thoroughly.
3. Cover chicken with the BBQ sauce mixture and simmer for 6-8 hours on low or 3-4 hours on high.
4. Fork-shred the cooked chicken.
5. Serve the shredded chicken and relish.

RECIPE 66

Ground Beef Stroganoff

For some who have trouble swallowing, a meat mixture made from thoroughly cooked ground beef, broth, and sour cream might be a welcome relief.

INGREDIENTS:

- 1 lb. ground beef
- ½ c. sour cream
- 1 c. beef broth
- ¼ c. minced onion
- 1 tsp. garlic powder
- Salt and pepper, as desired
- 1 packet of instant egg noodles

DIRECTIONS:

1. Prepare egg noodles per package directions and set aside.
2. Cook the ground beef in a hot skillet over a medium-high flame for a browned texture.
3. When the meat is done cooking, discard the fat left in the pan.
4. Put in a little sour cream, beef stock, chopped onion, garlic powder, salt, and pepper.
5. Simmer for 5-10 minutes once you've stirred everything together.
6. Enjoy your beef stroganoff with some egg noodles!

RECIPE 67

Stir-Fried Chicken and Vegetables

This is high in protein and vegetables, making it a healthy option for people with dysphagia who need a simple meal that is simple to swallow but still tastes great.

INGREDIENTS:

- 2 diced chicken breasts
- 1 c. chopped carrots
- 1 c. diced red and green peppers
- 1 c. zucchini slices
- 2 minced garlic cloves
- ½ c. water
- 1 tbsp. olive oil
- Salt and pepper, as desired

DIRECTIONS:

1. Prepare a large skillet by heating the olive oil over medium heat.
2. In a skillet, sauté the chicken cubes with the garlic until the chicken is cooked.
3. Take the chicken out of the pan and set it aside.
4. Put the sliced veggies in the pan and cook them until they're soft.
5. When you're done, put the chicken back in the pan and give it a good toss.
6. Put in as much salt and pepper as you like.
7. Serve warm, and enjoy!

RECIPE 68

Mashed Potatoes and Soft Meatballs

These high-protein and low-fuss meatballs and mashed potatoes are a great option for people with dysphagia since they are comforting and easy to eat, even if they have difficulty chewing or swallowing.

INGREDIENTS:

- 1 lb. ground beef
- ½ c. breadcrumbs
- 1 egg
- ¼ c. milk
- ¼ Grated parmesan cheese
- Salt and pepper, as desired
- 2 big potatoes, peeled and chopped

DIRECTIONS:

1. Start by preheating the oven to 375 degrees Fahrenheit (190 degrees Celsius).
2. Mix the ground meat, egg, bread crumbs, Parmesan cheese, milk, salt, and pepper in a bowl.
3. Combine all of the ingredients thoroughly.
4. Roll the dough into little meatballs and set them on an oven tray with parchment paper.
5. Put the meatballs in the oven and bake for 20 to 25 minutes.
6. Dice some potatoes and boil them until they're soft while the meatballs cook.
7. Remove the excess water from the potatoes, then mash them with butter, milk, salt, and pepper.
8. Place the tender meatballs atop a mound of mashed potatoes and dig in!

RECIPE 69

Avocado Toast with Soft Scrambled Eggs

This meal's high protein and healthy fat content make it an ideal breakfast choice for people with dysphagia.

INGREDIENTS:

- 2 big eggs
- 2 pieces of toast
- 1 mashed avocado
- 1 tbsp. butter
- Salt and pepper, as desired

DIRECTIONS:

1. Put some mashed avocado on toasted bread.
2. Put in as much salt and pepper as you like.
3. Slowly melt the butter in a small skillet.
4. Scramble the eggs until they're tender and creamy in a skillet.
5. Crumble the scrambled eggs over the avocado toast and savor.

RECIPE 70

Soft Meatloaf

This soft meatloaf is a high-protein and low-fuss recipe for anyone with dysphagia.

INGREDIENTS:

- 1 lb. ground beef
- ½ c. breadcrumbs
- ¼ c. milk
- 1 egg
- ¼ c. ketchup
- Salt and pepper, as desired

DIRECTIONS:

1. The oven needs to be heated to 375 degrees Fahrenheit (190 degrees Celsius).
2. Mix the ground meat, milk, bread crumbs, ketchup, egg, salt, and pepper in a bowl.
3. Combine all of the ingredients thoroughly.
4. Put the mixture in a prepared loaf pan and bake it.
5. Put the meatloaf in the oven and bake for 45-50 minutes.
6. Don't cut into the meatloaf immediately; give it a few minutes to cool.

RECIPE 71

Chicken Pot Pie

This dish's high protein and vegetable content makes it ideal for those with dysphagia who want a comfortable and easy-to-swallow dinner.

INGREDIENTS:

- 2 diced chicken breasts
- 1 c. mixed veggies, frozen
- ½ c. chicken broth
- ½ c. milk
- ¼ c. flour
- Salt and pepper, as desired
- 1 pie crust

DIRECTIONS:

1. The oven needs to be heated to 375 degrees Fahrenheit (190 degrees Celsius).
2. Brown and fully fry the chicken cubes in a large skillet.
3. Put the frozen vegetables in the pan and sauté them until they are soft.
4. To make the sauce, combine chicken broth, flour, milk, salt, and pepper in a separate bowl and whisk until smooth.
5. Put everything in the pan and mix it up.
6. Put the contents into a pie plate, then top with pie crust.
7. If you want a golden crust and piping hot filling in your chicken pot pie, bake it for 25 to 30 minutes.

RECIPES FOR SNACK AND DESSERTS

RECIPE 72

Banana Oatmeal Cookies

These cookies are a great snack for those with dysphagia because they are simple to chew and swallow. They have a lot of fiber and are naturally delicious.

INGREDIENTS:

- 2 ripe bananas, mashed
- 1 c. instant oatmeal
- ¼ c. raisins
- ¼ tsp. cinnamon

DIRECTIONS:

1. Set the oven's temperature to 350°F (175°C).
2. Mix the quick oats, raisins, cinnamon, and mashed bananas in a bowl.
3. Place heaping tablespoons of the batter on a baking sheet covered with parchment paper.
4. Bake the cookies for fifteen to twenty minutes until they are golden brown.
5. Before serving, allow the cookies to cool.

RECIPE 73

Yogurt Parfait

A yogurt parfait is a fantastic dessert for people with difficulty swallowing due to dysphagia because it is soft and easy to chew. Additionally, it contains a lot of fiber, protein, vitamins, and nutrients.

INGREDIENTS:

- 1 c. unsweetened Greek yogurt
- ½ c. strawberry slices
- ¼ c. granola
- Honey, as per taste preference

DIRECTIONS:

1. Place the Greek yogurt, strawberry slices, and granola in a small bowl.
2. Pour honey on top to increase sweetness.
3. Enjoy while serving chilled!

RECIPE 74

Chocolate Avocado Pudding

For those with dysphagia, this is a rich and simple-to-swallow dessert recipe. Additionally, it has a lot of fiber, antioxidants, and good fats.

INGREDIENTS:

- 2 Peeled and pitted ripe avocados.
- ½ c. unsweetened cocoa powder
- ½ c. almond milk
- ¼ c. honey
- 1 tsp. vanilla extract

DIRECTIONS:

1. Combine avocados peeled and pitted with honey, almond milk, cocoa powder, and the essence of vanilla in a blender.
2. Blend till creamy and smooth.
3. Before serving, let the pudding cool in the fridge for at least an hour.

RECIPE 75

Smoothie with Jelly and Peanut Butter

For those with dysphagia, this jelly with peanut butter smoothie recipe is a filling snack that is simple to swallow. It is a nutritious choice for any day because it is also rich in protein and good fats.

INGREDIENTS:

- 1 c. mixed frozen berries
- ½ c. almond milk
- ¼ c. peanut butter
- 1 tbsp. honey

DIRECTIONS:

1. Almond milk, honey, peanut butter, and assorted frozen berries should all be combined in a blender.
2. Blend till creamy and smooth.
3. Enjoy while serving chilled!

RECIPE 76

Apple Sauce with Cinnamon

People with dysphagia can have a tasty and nutritious snack with this recipe because it is simple to swallow. The cinnamon makes it taste better and has anti-inflammatory properties.

INGREDIENTS:

- 4 medium-sized chopped, cored, and peeled apples
- 1 tbsp. lemon juice
- ¼ tsp. Cinnamon
- ¼ c. water

DIRECTIONS:

1. Combine the lemon juice, sliced apples, cinnamon, and water in a big pot.
2. Cook the apples for 15 to 20 minutes over medium heat or until soft and tender.
3. The apple mixture should be smooth after being pureed using a hand-held blender or food processor.
4. Serving suggestions: Cool or room temperature.

RECIPE 77

Greek Yogurt with Almonds and Blueberries

Simple to chew and swallow. And it has a lot of fiber, protein, and antioxidants.

INGREDIENTS:

- 1 c. unsweetened Greek yogurt
- ½ c. Blueberries
- ¼ c. almond slices
- 1 tbsp. honey

DIRECTIONS:

1. Layer the blueberries, Greek yogurt, and sliced almonds in a small bowl.
2. Pour honey on top to increase sweetness.
3. Enjoy while serving chilled!

RECIPE 78

Chia Seed Pudding

A full and healthy snack for people with Dysphagia. Additionally, it has a lot of antioxidants, fiber, and omega-3 fatty acids.

INGREDIENTS:

- ¼ c. Chia seeds
- 1 c. almond milk
- 1 tbsp. Honey
- ½ tsp. vanilla extract
- Fresh fruits for toppings (optional)

DIRECTIONS:

1. Mix the almond milk, chia seeds, vanilla essence, and honey in a small bowl.
2. Stir the mixture occasionally as it chills in the fridge for at least two hours or overnight.
3. If preferred, top with fresh fruit and serve chilled.

RECIPE 79

Baked Cinnamon Apple Chips

Simple to chew and swallow. They are also higher in fiber and naturally sweeter than store-bought potato chips, making them a healthier option.

INGREDIENTS:

- 2 medium-sized apples, sliced very thin
- 1 tsp. cinnamon
- 1 tbsp. honey

DIRECTIONS:

1. Set the oven's temperature to 225°F (110°C).
2. Combine the honey and cinnamon in a small bowl.
3. On top of the thinly sliced apples, brush the mixture.
4. On a baking sheet covered with parchment paper, spread out the apples.
5. Bake the apples for two to three hours or until crispy.
6. At room temperature, dish out the apple chips.

RECIPE 80

Avocado Chocolate Mousse

This recipe for avocado chocolate mousse is a rich, creamy dessert that's simple to eat and contains beneficial fats from the avocado.

INGREDIENTS:

- 2 ripe avocados
- ¼ c. unsweetened cocoa powder
- ¼ c. honey
- ¼ c. Almond milk
- ½ tsp. vanilla extract

DIRECTIONS:

1. Blend the cocoa powder, honey, avocados, vanilla essence, and almond milk until well combined in a food processor.
2. At least one hour must pass before serving the mixture from the refrigerator.

RECIPE 81

Soft-Baked Oatmeal Cookies

These cookies are simple to chew and swallow. People with dysphagia can enjoy them as a snack or dessert. Additionally, because they contain fiber and good fats from the almond and oat flour, they are a healthier option for typical cookies.

INGREDIENTS:

- ½ c. old-fashioned oats
- ½ c. almond flour
- ½ c. unsweetened applesauce
- ¼ c. honey
- ¼ c. melted coconut oil
- 1 tsp. vanilla extract
- ½ tsp. baking soda
- ¼ tsp. salt

DIRECTIONS:

1. Set the oven's temperature to 350°F (175°C).
2. Combine the almond flour, oats, salt, and baking soda in a big pot.
3. Combine the honey, applesauce, vanilla extract, and coconut oil in another bowl.
4. Stir to thoroughly incorporate the dry ingredients before adding the wet ingredients.
5. Put spoonfuls of the dough on a baking sheet with attached parchment paper.
6. Bake the cookies for 10 to 12 mins or until they are brown.
7. Allow the cookies to cool completely on the baking pan before serving.

RECIPE 82

Mango Sorbet

Rich in antioxidants and vitamin C, this mango sorbet dish is a light and simple dessert.

INGREDIENTS:

- 2 ripe mangos, peeled and sliced
- ¼ c. honey
- ¼ c. water
- 1 tbsp. lime juice

DIRECTIONS:

1. Blend the honey, mangoes, lime juice, and water until completely smooth in a food processor.
2. Put it in a jar that can go in the freezer and stir it occasionally for 4 hours.
3. Serve the sorbet right away after scooping it into tiny dishes.

RECIPE 83

Soft-Cooked Poached Pears

These soft-cooked, poached pears are a delicious and fragrant treat full of antioxidants and fiber. They are also simple to consume.

INGREDIENTS:

- 2 ripe pears, peeled and halved
- ½ c. orange juice
- ¼ c. honey
- 1 stick of cinnamon

DIRECTIONS:

1. Bring the honey, cinnamon stick, and orange juice to a simmer in a small saucepan.
2. The sliced pears should be added to the pot and simmered for 15 to 20 mins or until tender.
3. The poached pears can be served warm or cold.

RECIPE 84

Chocolate Pudding

This recipe has a creamy, smooth, and palatable texture. Additionally, it has plenty of protein and calcium.

INGREDIENTS:

- ½ c. sugar
- ¼ c. unsweetened cocoa powder
- 3 tbsp. cornstarch
- ⅛ tsp. salt
- 2 c. milk
- 1 tsp. vanilla extract

DIRECTIONS:

1. Mix the cocoa powder, sugar, salt, and cornstarch in a medium saucepan.
2. As you whisk the milk in, the mixture will become smooth.
3. Cook until the mixture thickens and boils while whisking continuously over medium heat.
4. Add vanilla extract after turning the heat off.
5. Refrigerate the pudding until it is set, then pour it into a serving dish or separate cup.

RECIPE 85

Mango Yogurt Smoothie

This recipe's smooth and drinking texture is ideal for those with dysphagia. It is also a good way to get probiotics and vitamin C.

INGREDIENTS:

- 1 mango, peeled and sliced
- ½ c. vanilla yogurt
- ½ c. milk

DIRECTIONS:

1. Blend each item separately in a blender until completely smooth.
2. Serve right away.

RECIPE 86
Fruit Salad

This recipe's soft and chewy texture is ideal for those with dysphagia. Additionally, it is an excellent source of fiber and vitamin C.

INGREDIENTS:

- 1 c. chopped strawberries
- 1 c. diced pineapple
- 1 c. diced kiwi
- 1 c. diced mango
- ¼ c. orange juice

DIRECTIONS:

1. In a big bowl, mix everything.
2. Refrigerate.
3. Serve cold

RECIPE 87

Apple Slices Baked

This recipe's soft and easily swallowed texture is ideal for those with dysphagia. Additionally, it has a lot of antioxidants and fiber.

INGREDIENTS:

- 2 apples, cored and sliced
- 1 tbsp. melted butter
- ¼ tsp. cinnamon
- 1 tsp. honey

DIRECTIONS:

1. Preheat the oven to 350 degrees Fahrenheit.
2. Honey, cinnamon, and melted butter should all be combined in a small basin.
3. Spread the sliced apple slices in a single layer on a baking sheet with parchment paper underneath.
4. Apply the butter mixture on the apple slices with a brush.
5. Bake the apples for 15 to 20 mins or until they are delicate and soft.
6. Serve hot.

RECIPES FOR BEVERAGES

RECIPE 88

Strawberry-Banana Smoothie

With a smooth, easy-to-swallow texture, this smoothie makes it simple to get your daily amount of fruit and dairy.

INGREDIENTS:

- 1 sliced banana
- 1 c. frozen strawberries
- ½ c. vanilla Greek yogurt
- ½ c. milk or milk substitute
- 1 tbsp. Honey (optional)

DIRECTIONS:

1. Blend each item separately in a blender until completely smooth.
2. If required, add extra milk to thin out the consistency.
3. Offer chilled.

RECIPE 89

Chocolate Almond Milk

For people who are lactose intolerant, this beverage offers a lactose-free alternative and a delectable, chocolatey flavor.

INGREDIENTS:

- 1 c. unsweetened almond milk
- 1 tbsp. unsweetened cocoa powder
- 1 tbsp. Honey (or other preferred sweeteners)

DIRECTIONS:

1. Blend each item separately in a blender until completely smooth.
2. Offer cold.

RECIPE 90

Creamy Vanilla Shake

Traditional delight with a creamy, delicious texture that is neither overly thick nor challenging to consume.

INGREDIENTS:

- 1 c. vanilla (or other flavors) ice cream
- ½ c. milk or milk substitute
- ½ tsp. vanilla extract

DIRECTIONS:

1. Blend each item separately in a blender until completely smooth.
2. Offer cold.

RECIPE 91

Pineapple Coconut Water

The combination of pineapple sweetness and honey makes this hydrated and nourishing beverage a delectable treat for people with dysphagia.

INGREDIENTS:

- 1 c. coconut water
- ½ c. frozen pineapple chunks
- 1 tsp. lime juice
- 1 tbsp. Honey (or other preferred sweeteners)

DIRECTIONS:

1. Blend each item separately in a blender until completely smooth.
2. Offer cold.

RECIPE 92

Apple Cinnamon Smoothie

This smoothie has a flavor mix of sweet and spicy and is a healthy source of fiber and protein.

INGREDIENTS:

- 1 peeled and diced apple
- ½ c. plain Greek yogurt
- ½ c. unsweetened applesauce
- ½ tsp. cinnamon powder
- ½ c. milk or milk substitute

DIRECTIONS:

1. Blend each item separately in a blender until completely smooth.
2. If required, add extra milk to thin out the consistency.
3. Offer chilled.

RECIPE 93
Blueberry Green Tea

It offers a revitalizing and antioxidant-rich alternative for people with dysphagia.

INGREDIENTS:

- 1 c. chilled, brewed green tea
- ½ c. frozen blueberries
- 1 tbsp. Honey (or other preferred sweeteners)

DIRECTIONS:

1. Blend each item separately in a blender until completely smooth.
2. Offer chilled.

RECIPE 94

Vanilla Chai Latte

This latte offers people with dysphagia a warm, soothing alternative in addition to the health advantages of tea and honey.

INGREDIENTS:

- 1 c. milk or milk substitute
- 1 chai tea bag
- ½ tsp. vanilla extract
- 1 tbsp. Honey (or other preferred sweeteners)

DIRECTIONS:

1. Heat milk over a moderate flame in a saucepan until it is warm but not boiling.
2. Stepping a tea bag of chai in boiling milk for three to five minutes.
3. Take out the tea bag, then add the honey and vanilla extract.
4. Serve warm.

RECIPE 95

Orange Creamsicle Smoothie

This smoothie is a fantastic protein and vitamin C source with a nostalgic and energizing flavor.

INGREDIENTS:

- 1 orange, chopped after peeling
- ½ c. vanilla Greek yogurt
- ½ c. milk or milk substitute
- ½ tsp. vanilla extract

DIRECTIONS:

1. Blend each item separately in a blender until completely smooth.
2. If required, add extra milk to thin out the consistency.
3. Offer cold.

RECIPE 96

Iced Herbal Tea

Provides a cooling and comforting beverage for people with Dysphagia. Teas made from herbs are frequently used as medicines because they can relieve inflammation and digestive problems.

INGREDIENTS:

- 1 herbal tea bag (such as peppermint, chamomile, or ginger)
- 1 c. hot water
- 1 c. ice
- Honey or sugar, if desired

DIRECTIONS:

- 1 herbal tea bag (such as peppermint, chamomile, or ginger)
- 1 c. hot water
- 1 c. ice
- Honey or sugar, if desired

RECIPE 97

Homemade Sports Drink

The electrolytes in this DIY sports drink are easily replaced, which is helpful for those with dysphagia. The body's fluid and mineral equilibrium is restored by sugar and salt.

INGREDIENTS:

- 2 tbsp. sugar
- ⅛ tsp. salt
- 2 tbsp. lemon juice
- 1 c. water

DIRECTIONS:

1. Sugar and salt should be thoroughly mixed in a small bowl.
2. Combine the lemon juice and water in a glass or water bottle.
3. Stir in the sugar-salt mixture after adding it.

RECIPE 98

Creamy Coconut Milkshake

People with dysphagia will enjoy the creamy coconut milkshake since it is so tasty. The beneficial lipids in coconut milk might aid digestion and reduce inflammation.

INGREDIENTS:

- ½ c. coconut milk
- ½ c. vanilla ice cream
- ¼ c. crushed ice

DIRECTIONS:

1. Blend the vanilla ice cream, coconut milk, and ice cubes in a blender.
2. Blend till creamy and smooth.

RECIPE 99

Carrot Ginger Juice

For those with dysphagia, this juice is a filling and tasty beverage. While ginger can aid digestion and reduce inflammation, carrots are high in vitamins and minerals.

INGREDIENTS:

- 1-inch piece of fresh ginger peeled and diced
- 2 medium-sized carrots, peeled and chopped
- ½ c. water
- Honey (optional)

DIRECTIONS:

1. Combine the ginger, carrots, and water in a blender.
2. Blend until completely smooth.
3. Juice should be filtered using cheesecloth or a sieve with fine mesh.
4. If desired, taste and add honey.

RECIPE 100

Creamy Mango Lassi

Those who struggle to swallow thicker drinks due to dysphagia would benefit greatly from this creamy mango lassi. Also, it's easier to swallow.

INGREDIENTS:

- 1 peeled and sliced ripe mango
- 1 c. plain yogurt
- ½ c. milk
- 1 tbsp. Honey
- ¼ tsp. cardamom powder

DIRECTIONS:

1. Add the mango chunks, milk, yogurt, cardamom, and honey to a blender.
2. Blend till creamy and smooth.
3. Pour into a glass, then serve right away.

CHAPTER 8

4-WEEK MEAL PLAN

Meal planning for people with dysphagia? That's about as interesting as eating a bowl of porridge. Don't worry, though, since I'm here to disprove your assumptions. Sure, the thought of a diet for dysphagia may bring unappealing, flavorless purees to mind. But what if I told you that you could still have tasty and healthy meals without sacrificing convenience or taste?

That's right, guys. Dysphagia patients, prepare to have your world turned upside down by this four-week meal plan. So, what exactly does this diet entail? Prepare to bid farewell to tasteless purees and welcome in a world of variety. Everything from tender meats to properly cooked veggies is blended to a silky smooth consistency, making them a breeze to consume.

But don't worry; this diet isn't about blending everything you see. We'll use various flavors and textures to add some spice. Take your pick from delicious oatmeal recipes that will make you forget you're eating a bowl of morning cereal, quinoa pieces that are both soft and chewy, and roasted chickpeas with just the right amount of crunch.

Also, let's not forget the sweets. A person's inability to swallow should not prevent them from enjoying a tasty treat. We have everything you might want, from tangy sorbets to silky pudding. Take your dysphagia meals to the next level with this culinary getaway I'm about to take you on by blending some of your favorite foods. I am confident that your patients, and their taste buds, will appreciate your efforts.

Note: Please keep in mind that these are only ballpark figures and that your specific calorie requirements may vary based on factors like your age, gender, degree of activity, and health. It is essential to get the advice of a qualified medical practitioner to design a tailored diet plan. Before we get started, it's important to remember that individual patients' needs may differ, so it's recommended to visit a healthcare provider or a qualified dietitian to ensure the diet plan is appropriate for the patient's condition. Dysphagia patients should also focus on texture adjustments like pureeing or finely cutting food. So, with that in mind, check out this sample 4-week diet plan:

Week 1

Day	Breakfast	Lunch	Dinner	Calories
1	Easy, Delicious, & Creamy Scrambled Eggs	Cream of mushroom soup, pureed roasted sweet potato	Gravy-flavored chicken breast puree, mashed carrots, and turnips	1300-1600
2	Pureed oatmeal with honey and chopped blueberries, pureed mango	Pureed roasted zucchini, pureed tomato soup	Pureed salmon with lemon and herb seasoning, pureed green beans	1300-1600
3	Pureed peaches, honey-sweetened Greek yogurt with chopped nuts	Broccoli and split pea soup, both pureed	Vegetables and beef in a pureed stew with mashed potatoes	1300-1600
4	Fruit smoothie made from cottage cheese, strawberries, and pineapple juice	Pureed asparagus and butternut squash soup	Meatloaf with roasted Brussels sprouts blended	1300-1600
5	Pancakes topped with pureed blueberries and maple syrup	Black bean and roasted cauliflower soups pureed	Chicken and dumplings, pureed mixed vegetables	1300-1600
6	Pureed orange, spinach, and feta omelet	Soup with broccoli and cheddar, roasted beets pureed	Apple sauce, carrots, and peas pureed pork chops	1300-1600
7	Cinnamon roll oats, pear puree	Potato-leek soup, steaming green beans.	Roasted sweet potato, parsnip, and turkey blended with gravy.	1300-1600

Week 2

Day	Breakfast	Lunch	Dinner	Calories
1	Scrambled eggs with cheddar and banana puree	Roasted sweet potato and chicken noodle soup.	Pureed green beans and beef stroganoff	1300-1600
2	Honeyed blueberry yogurt, mango puree	Roasted zucchini puree, tomato bisque	Pureed fish, carrots, and turnips	1300-1600
3	Peaches and pineapple pureed cottage cheese	Pureed steamed broccoli and cauliflower soup	Pureed mashed potatoes and pork tenderloin	1300-1600
4	Pureed orange juice, raisins, and brown sugar in an oatmeal cinnamon swirl	Roasted asparagus puree, split pea soup	Roasted Brussels sprouts and gravy-puréed meatballs	1300-1600
5	Pureed apple and blueberry pancakes	Pureed steaming green beans and butternut squash soup	Mushroom-sauced chicken and sweet potato purée	1300-1600
6	Omelet with pureed spinach and feta, pureed pear	Roasted beets and broccoli-cheese soup.	Pureed carrots, peas, and beef pot roast with gravy	1300-1600
7	Spinach and cheese scrambled eggs, peach puree	Pureed roasted sweet potato and cream of mushroom soup	Pureed cauliflower and turkey meatballs	1300-1600

Week 3

Day	Breakfast	Lunch	Dinner	Calories
1	Strawberry-honey oatmeal, mango puree	Chicken-vegetable soup and grilled zucchini puree	Roast beef, mashed carrots, and turnips	1300-1600
2	Blueberry-honey cottage cheese, apple puree	Pureed steamed asparagus and broccoli and cheese soup	Herb-seasoned pureed chicken and sweet potato	1300-1600
3	Peach-almond yogurt and pineapple puree	Roasted beets and tomato soup blended	Apple-sauced pork chops and mashed potatoes	1300-1600
4	Pureed orange and cinnamon oatmeal with raisins	Steamed broccoli and split pea soup pureed	Roasted Brussels sprouts and lemon-dill salmon puree	1300-1600
5	Pureed pear and blueberry pancakes	Butternut squash and cauliflower soup	Blended meatloaf, mashed potatoes, and mashed carrots and peas	1300-1600
6	Omelet with pureed spinach and feta, pureed pear	Roasted beets and broccoli-cheese soup.	Pureed carrots, peas, and beef pot roast with gravy	1300-1600
7	Scrambled eggs with cheddar and peach puree	Pureed steaming green beans and cream of mushroom soup	Pureed turkey and potatoes	1300-1600

Week 4

Day	Breakfast	Lunch	Dinner	Calories
1	Avocado egg salad	Risotto with butternut squash	Red sauce meatballs	1300-1600
2	Strawberry-almond yogurt, apple puree	Tomato bisque and grilled asparagus	Pureed sweet potato and salmon patties	1300-1600
3	Pureed cottage cheese and peaches or pineapple and honey	Roasted beets and broccoli-cheese soup	Pork tenderloin and cauliflower purée	1300-1600
4	Pureed orange juice, raisins, and brown sugar in an oatmeal cinnamon swirl	Stir-fried chicken and vegetables	Chicken and rice with cream sauce	1300-1600
5	Pancakes topped with pureed pear and blueberries served with maple syrup	Pureed steaming green beans and butternut squash soup	Gravy-coated meatballs	1300-1600
6	Salad with Shredded Chicken	Roasted sweet potato puree and cauliflower soup	Roast beef and green beans	1300-1600
7	Pureed peach, scrambled eggs, and cheddar cheese	Pureed steaming green beans and cream of mushroom soup	Pureed turkey and potatoes	1300-1600

CONCLUSION

Hey, good job, you read all the way through! We hope you find our Dysphagia Cookbook helpful in overcoming your swallowing challenges. If you're having trouble swallowing, this book will give you the confidence to eat again by providing healthy and delicious meals.

Having trouble swallowing can be irritating, especially if it keeps us from eating the things we love. Our Dysphagia Cookbook will show you that flavor and texture don't have to be mutually exclusive. We offer a wide selection of mouthwatering and manageable dishes. Our cookbook has something for everyone, from hearty stews to delicious smoothies.

There's more, though. If you want to help a loved one who is having trouble swallowing, our Dysphagia Cookbook is a fantastic tool for you to use. To ensure the health and happiness of your loved ones, use our cookbook to create delectable dishes you can feel confident serving. Our recipes are simple to follow and come with useful hints on how to tailor them to each person's preferences.

Our Dysphagia Cookbook stands out from the crowd in part because of the wide range of dishes it covers. We've included recipes suitable for various diets and tastes because no two people are alike. Everyone can find something they like in our cookbook, whether they prefer vegetarian or meat-based food.

Our core philosophy in creating this Dysphagia Cookbook is that everyone, regardless of their physical abilities, should be able to enjoy eating. We believe that food is more than just fuel; it can also provide us with great pleasure and solace. This is why we've put so much effort into developing digestible, tasty, and filling meals.

We appreciate you buying our Dysphagia Cookbook and hope you enjoy it. If you've been having trouble swallowing, we hope this will assist, and if you're open to trying new foods, we hope this will inspire you. Remember that food is not just necessary for survival; it may also bring great pleasure. Now that our confidence is up, let's get into the kitchen and start making tasty dishes!

REFERENCES

Bhattacharyya, N. (2014). The Prevalence of Dysphagia among Adults in the United States. *Otolaryngology–Head and Neck Surgery, 151*(5), 765–769. https://doi.org/10.1177/0194599814549156

National Institute on Deafness & Other Communication Disorders. (2017, March 6). *What Is Dysphagia (Difficulty Swallowing)? | NIDCD.* Www.nidcd.nih.gov. https://www.nidcd.nih.gov/health/dysphagia#7

Wolf, D. C. (1990). *Dysphagia* (H. K. Walker, W. D. Hall, & J. W. Hurst, Eds.). PubMed; Butterworths. https://www.ncbi.nlm.nih.gov/books/NBK408/#:~:text=Dysphagia%20can%20be%20classified%20into